Doing Business with John

*Start and Build a Successful Business Organization
Based on the Example of Jesus in the Book of John*

E. L. Parker

DOING BUSINESS WITH JOHN

How to Start and Build a Successful Business Organization
Based on Christ's Example in the Book of John

E.L. Parker

Edited By A. Houck

Library of Congress Cataloging-in-Publication Data
Parker, E.L.
  Doing Business with John: How to Start and Build a
  Successful Business Organization Based on Christ's
  Example in the Book of John / by E.L. Parker

ISBN 0-9770778-0-2

Cover designed by Art Cruz

Published By
The Marketing Company
PO Box 8394 Redlands, CA 92375
www.tmcwebsite.com

Praise God, He wrote this book first!

Dedicated to my wife, children and church.
All of them make life worth living

Introduction

For some time, I have pondered a question for the American church in general. Pastors, missionary teams and others will go to the poorest and most dangerous parts of any American city to save souls and share the word of Jesus Christ. Those who do should be admired because they face danger, rejection and the heartbreak of seeing the pain and suffering of the poor and forgotten. There are others who work in hospitals and nursing homes, areas in which their efforts are also greatly needed. When we travel to these locations, we pass hundreds, if not thousands, of small to large businesses that are filled with potential believers who are also worthy of our ministry efforts.

Right or wrong, I believe that pastors and church staff may have formed opinions and made the following judgments regarding business people:

1. Business people appear organized, prosperous and stable, therefore they do not need ministry effort.

2. Business people are busy and shouldn't be interrupted.

3. Business people are smarter than us, so why should they listen to what we have to say?

4. The business that they are engaged in is immoral and not worth our effort.

5. We have nothing in common. Business and the bible don't mix.

With those thoughts in mind, I set about to write a book that can be used to explain to business people (owners, managers and employees) how God's word can be a blueprint for business and organizational growth. This book was also written to give those in the ministry information on how the bible relates to business people so they may have a dialogue with them.

It is critical that the American church make business outreach part of their ministry. In this group of people are the future leaders and supporters of the church. The people who know how to organize, budget and oversee projects are the future of church growth and prosperity and are waiting to hear their invitation to be part of God's ministry.

To start with, let me state that I do not consider myself to be an expert in business or scripture. My background is primarily in the sales and business management areas. In 1994, I left a sales and marketing management position with a "Fortune 80" corporation to start a marketing and management company that worked primarily with small to medium sized manufacturing and service related business owners. Working with limited self-education and previous business experience, I set out to advise a client base that was equally uneducated from a formal standpoint, but very effective in getting the job done on a daily basis. I found this work to be exciting, depressing, educational and worthwhile. It amazed me (and still does) just how much strength is found in this part of the American business culture and how much effort and blessing it takes to survive and prosper in this free market arena.

In my initial analysis with clients, I would help them to determine where they wanted to go, what needed to be done to get there and identify what has been stopping them from achieving their goals up to that point.

In addressing these business goals with each client, I was able to see how much of an impact their personal opinions had on their business. Many times, like all of us, they would say things that did not match their actions, regarding production goals, employee relations, market share, business growth, etc. The clients who really did want to succeed did so every time. Others spoke of wanting success and happiness, but when it started to come as a result of their planning, they retreated from it as if they feared the changes that it brought. I attribute this reaction to several factors, including a lack of formal business education, no written guideline of business rules that they could trust, and an insufficient sense of how much success they were allowed to have.

During the initial business evaluation, I met with each employee to evaluate his or her views towards business management and ownership. While I consulted with the business owners and managers from the planning side, I met with each employee to ascertain if the planning we had put in place was working. I started with an introductory employee interview and asked simple questions that related to how they viewed things from an employee standpoint. In almost all cases, I found that ownership, management and employees viewed the same issues and ideas radically different. If ownership saw production goals as a way to survive, middle management saw those same goals as unattainable. The employees used those goals to set their own production rhythms so that they could have as many hours as possible on their paychecks that week. The common thread was a profound distrust for those above, in the middle and below. Without a standard to measure, how are we to behave as employers, managers and employees? Left to our own devices, the way to establish healthy working relationships is confusing. The good news is that through God and His word we have very clear rules and guidelines.

One of the most influential secular books I have read is "In Search of Excellence" by Tom Peters. I recommend this book to people whenever I can and after more than twenty years, it is still relevant. Its simple message is biblical in nature: if you are going to do something, do it with excellence. Be the best employee, business owner, spouse, citizen, parent, child, whatever role you have. Give it your best effort.

Reading the first Book of John, I realized that Jesus gave us a strategy on how to build an organization from the ground up. From John the

Baptist doing the work of pre-publicity and marketing to the point that Jesus took off to build a management team. He eventually brought in an outsider, Paul the Apostle, who was uniquely gifted to deliver the message far beyond its initial market to an ever-expanding worldwide marketplace. God did all of this from a total "startup" mode and gave us a clear, concise blueprint for success to follow. From zero to two billion members that represent almost 33% of the earth's population, not only has the church grown and prospered, it continues to grow in places like Africa and Asia. Growth is so strong that it is forecasted that China could be a Christian nation in the next twenty-five years.

If you are a believer, you may already see how this important book of the bible can offer you encouragement and insight into business and personal success. If you are not a believer yet, now is as good as any time to get to know who our Lord is and what He is about.

To those of you who may read this book with an eye on a business ministry, you will be rewarded not only spiritually, but you will also see practical and positive results for your church and ministry. Business people are achievers, they have vision and energy and they love, in most cases, to meet goals they have set for themselves. All of these qualities can help a church and ministry grow to meet the physical and spiritual needs of its community.

I hope that you enjoy this book and may you be blessed in all that you do.

Chapter One

*O*n chapter one, the bible tells us that Jesus is the eternal Word, that He has been with the Father since the beginning and that His life gives light to everyone. The bible then tells us in chapter one that God sent John the Baptist to tell everyone about the light so that they all might believe, because of his testimony. Although the world in general may not recognize Him, and His own people may reject Him, those who did believe in Him were given the right to be children of God.

In reading about John the Baptist, I am struck by his qualities of loyalty, leadership and submission to authority. In Chapter 1:6, the bible says that God sent John to tell everyone about Jesus, that by his testimony others would believe and that he was a true witness to the fact that Jesus was the light of the world. In the first chapter of John, John the Baptist gave a true third party testimony as to who Christ was and is. He knew that God had promised His people in Exodus 6:6-8 that He would do three things for the people of Israel:

1. Bring them out of captivity.
2. Make them free.
3. Offer them redemption.

Based on these and other prophetic promises, John the Baptist recognized Jesus to be the promised Messiah and felt confident to pronounce His coming to everyone. If God had not already delivered on previous promises, John the Baptist would not have been able to recognize Jesus as the Redeemer. The pre-publicity role that John the Baptist played was essential for the future success of Christ's ministry.

Another great business lesson the Book of John teaches is where to look for key members of your organization, how to engage them and how to bring them onboard. Jesus didn't wait for key people; He went out and found them. Chapter 1:37-39 tells us that the first two disciples immediately followed Christ after meeting Him and that they went to where He was staying and hung out together. I don't know about you, but I think that must have been an interesting conversation with the Lord. I can just imagine Andrew making small talk: "So, have you been in town long?" In verses 40-41, the bible tells us that Andrew went to find his brother Simon Peter. He told him that he had found the Messiah and then brought him to Jesus. Another example of how Jesus assembled His core group is detailed in John 1:43. In that verse, it says that Jesus got up that morning and went to Galilee, where He found Philip. The practical value in this verse is that Jesus knew that He wanted Philip to be part of his organization and He pursued him instead of waiting for Philip to find Him.

When Jesus put His organization together, He was driven by a love for what He was doing and He knew who He wanted to do business with. It was equally important that His disciples were looking for Him. In verse 1:40, Andrew went to his brother Peter and said, "We have found the Messiah". In John 1:45, Philip went to find Nathaniel and told him, "We have found the very person Moses and the prophets wrote about". The apostles were earnestly looking for Jesus as much as He was looking for them. They were looking for prophecy to be fulfilled and Jesus was looking for them to fulfill the prophecy.

Another hurdle that the Lord overcame in the building of His organization was how to endure negative people and their preconceived opinions of who you are and where you come from. In John 1:45, when Philip went to look for Nathaniel to tell him about finding Jesus, Nathaniel's response was negative because Philip told him that Jesus came from Nazareth. "Can anything good come from (Nazareth) there?," asked Nathaniel. We judge, and are judged by, everyone on the basis of what they (we) look like and where they (we) come from. Even though Nathaniel questioned if anything good could come from Nazareth, he stuck around to meet Jesus and made the decision that He was the Messiah, a decision that his future depended on.

Chapter One Business Lesson

I don't know too many small business owners who start with pre-publicity and effective advertising that aims to tell the world about the good things that are going to happen for them when they open their doors. By the same token, I don't know of one large company that fails to trumpet their message prior to the time they are ready to do business.

A good corporate example of this would be AutoZone, a national auto parts retailer that opened its first store in Forrest City, Arkansas, in 1979. The business started under the name Auto Shack and changed its business name in 1987. They currently have over 3,000 locations. It wasn't until the late 1990's that AutoZone actually made the transition from a regional company to a national company. Even though they were not in every marketplace, they advertised on a nationwide basis. I live in Southern California and knew quite a bit about AutoZone long before the opened a store near me.

Just as important as the message is, consider the media that you use to deliver it. Does your message have integrity? Is it embellished? Does the medium used have integrity? Using the standards of John the Baptist is a real challenge because they are exceedingly high. John the Baptist was very clear regarding who Jesus was and felt confident to announce to the world his belief.

The AutoZone example of brand development was based primarily on broad television and radio advertising that is expensive and prohibitive for a small business startup. Because they were trying to crash an existing, mature and competitive marketplace, the company banked on the repetitive nature of this form of advertising to establish a name brand that would have high recognition with customers before a store was placed in their neighborhood.

All of this brand development would have been wasted if AutoZone didn't follow through and build those stores nationwide. From Genesis to Malachi, God gave us advance notice that He was sending a savior to redeem us. By using this pre-publicity, we knew where He would be born, what family He would be descended from, what His ministry would be about and most importantly, why He would come in the first place. This was important to do, so that we would be able to recognize Him when He came. I wonder if AutoZone was even aware that their marketing plan had biblical origins?

When Jesus started His ministry, he didn't wait for His startup management team to find Him, He went looking for them. The thing that qualified them was the fact that they knew scripture and they were in fact keeping an eye out for the Messiah. Jesus knew his market and went out to find it. He didn't sit back and wait for them to find Him. God used effective pre-event publicity to promote the coming of Jesus all through history and sent John the Baptist to take care of the final details so that it would be impossible to miss who He was and the fact that scripture was indeed being fulfilled. John the Baptist was straightforward and truthful in his message and he did an excellent job preparing the Christian base. Jesus made his managerial selections based on the personal qualities of each apostle and their future potential, rather than who or what they were at the time He met them. He didn't discriminate in regard to where they came from or their social standing, but instead on what they would become. He also spent time talking and listening in order to really get to know them. Let's face it, the best educated and most powerful people did not follow Jesus at this time as they had too much to lose to be part of a "startup" operation and their existing social and community stature was not transferable.

When we build a business organization, it is best to recruit people who share our values and interests. It is also very important that they value their involvement and accomplishments beyond monetary rewards. Everyone needs to pay their bills and everyone has a need for money, but it is just as important that they share your passion for what they are doing. It is very possible that they are looking for you and your product or service and have potential markets and uses that you may have never thought of.

One day, while driving to an appointment, I heard an interview on the radio. The man being interviewed was regarded as one of the most successful of modern day inventors. He was, and is, a success by any business standards. The interviewer asked him to relate which one of his many hundreds of inventions was the most financially successful. The man quickly explained that he loved classical music and, because the natural oil on his hands would transfer to the record and possibly affect its future integrity, he invented an envelope cover that would allow him to place the record on the turntable and never have to touch his precious records again. The interviewer haltingly asked, "That is your most successful invention? I can't say that I have ever heard of it before." The inventor answered by saying that he had zero sales of his "record envelopes" but that another man saw his patent and applied its design principles to the personal computer. That is how the floppy disk was invented, of which the inventor receives a royalty for each one sold.

In regard to the question from Nathaniel, about the value of someone from a particular place, educational background or of a certain race, please consider the following example.

George Washington Carver was born in 1864 near Diamond Grove, Missouri, on the farm of Moses Carver. When he was a baby, he and his mother were kidnapped by Confederate night raiders and were believed to have been sent away to Arkansas. Moses Carver reclaimed George after the Civil War but his mother had disappeared forever. His father was never identified, so Moses and Susan Carver raised George and his brother as their own children. With a natural sense of discovery, George spent a great deal of his childhood keenly interested in plants and rocks. George made every effort to receive a formal education. He worked as a farm hand in the southwest part of Missouri and attended a one -room schoolhouse. Later, he was accepted as the first black student at Simpson College in Indianola, Iowa, where he studied piano and art. He transferred to Iowa Agricultural College (now Iowa State University) in 1891, received his Bachelor of Science degree in 1894 and a Master of Science degree in 1897. He became the first Black faculty member at Iowa State College of Agriculture and Mechanics and taught about soil conservation and related agricultural subjects. In 1897, the founder of the Tuskegee Normal and Industrial Institute for Negroes, Booker T. Washington, invited him to join the faculty as the school's Director of Agriculture, where he remained until his death in 1943.

George was prolific in regard to the discoveries he made throughout his career. Many of these discoveries are used everyday and include mayonnaise, meat tenderizer, metal polish, paper, plastic, pavement, shaving cream, shoe polish, synthetic rubber, talcum powder, wood stain, adhesives, axle grease, bleach, buttermilk, chili sauce, fuel briquettes, ink, instant coffee and linoleum. The biggest impact he made on the world was the "crop rotation" method of farming. The economy of the South was directly related to the farming of soil depleting crops like cotton. He proposed the alternate planting of soil enriching crops like peanuts, peas, soybeans, sweet potatoes and pecans. His discoveries and theories were directly related to the recovery of Southern agriculture after the Civil War.

Everything that George Washington Carver accomplished was driven by his love for God and his fellow man. He did not patent or profit from most of his inventions and he freely gave his discoveries to mankind. He would say about his ideas and inventions, "God gave them to me, how can I sell them to someone else?" On his grave is the epitaph:

He could have added fortune to fame, but caring for neither, he found happiness and honor in being helpful to the world

The great irony of George Washington Carver's life is that he was born during a period of repression and the very people who repressed him benefited greatly from his ideas and inventions. Imagine the reaction of the first cotton farmer, involved in a business decimated by soil depleting farming methods, war and general chaos of the times. Along comes George Washington Carver with his theories of crop rotation that could save the farming industry across the entire South. Can you imagine that farmer looking at that black man and wondering, "What good could come from him and his ideas? Why should I take the advice of a slave who wants to help me and wants nothing in return?" As it turns out, it's a good thing that the agricultural community listened to the advice because their future depended on it.

Like Nathaniel, that farmer had to determine that, yes; something good could come from Nazareth. In business, like in life, choose your associates based on shared Godly values. Find people who are looking for what you are looking for and take the time to get to know them. If you are a startup business or organization, make an effort to go and speak to people about your goals and visions. See if there are not only good potential co-laborers who share your dream, but also customers who need your product or service. Don't prejudge or preclude any potential staff member or customer based on their demographics, as both have to be developed over time.

Questions:

1. If you were able to be a prolific inventor like George Washington Carver, would you have given away your inventions without compensation? Why? What would your friends and family say if you did? From what perspective would a business magazine write a story about you if you did?

2. Have you, or how would you, go about building your business management team? How does it compare to the examples used by Jesus in this chapter?

Notes

Notes

Chapter Two

$\mathcal{I}$n the second chapter of John, there are three great lessons to be learned and applied to our daily business life. One of those lessons involves listening to the advice of others pertaining to timing and opportunity. The bible states that at the wedding feast at Cana, Jesus listened to Mary's advice and started moving forward with His ministry even when He did not initially think it was the time to do so. He trusted His Mother and if it was not truly the time to make that move, He wouldn't have done it. Our loved ones see us from a different perspective. Because they love us and want us to succeed, they can point out opportunities that we may fail to see. I believe it is important to note that their advice could also relate to the dangers and pitfalls on the road to business success. In business, as in life, we have to use those around us to temper our pessimism and optimism and help keep us balanced.

After the first public miracle at the wedding feast, the bible tell us that Jesus went away to spend some time with His family and apostles. I have known many successful businesspeople that didn't take the time to rest, reflect and enjoy what God has given them. Make renewal, reflection and rest a part of your business plan.

The third lesson of this chapter is found in the clearing of the temple. Many people, myself included, have had this vision of Jesus walking into the temple and going bonkers, flipping over tables, chairs and people. Instead of displaying a spontaneous and quick temper, the bible says that Jesus took His time and braided a whip before taking action. Our Lord knew what He was doing and took the time to formulate a plan of action based on truth and sound biblical reasoning. He may not have looked organized to those on the receiving end of His action, but this incident was essential to His projected goals.

Chapter Two Business Lesson

If you are starting a business or manage an existing business or organization, let those around you have access to your dreams, values and goals. Remember, in the previous chapter we discussed how to select a staff and develop confidential partners and advisors. It is best to listen to the advice of a person who has something to gain or lose by the decision they are advising you on. When Jesus listened to Mary's advice regarding His ministry, He knew that Mary had just as much at stake as Jesus did. At the time of the Immaculate Conception, Mary became the first person to accept Christ spiritually and physically. Mary played a big part in the life and ministry of Jesus because of her acceptance of God's plan. As an advisor, Jesus knew that Mary's word was golden. He trusted her intuition and knew that they were on the same page. If you will notice, Jesus didn't turn to the apostles and ask for a show of hands regarding the issue of the first miracle. Jesus knew that the men that He had picked for His startup management team had the potential to be strong leaders and advisors somewhere in the future. At that particular moment, only one person was worthy to be listened to, one who had the credentials and shared investment in His ministry.

Often I dealt with companies that had owners and managers who listened to bad managerial advice. In corporate America I watched more than one CEO get a hair-brained idea for a product or service that had no chance of being successful. They went ahead with it anyway because they were surrounded with people who agreed with them, even though they knew the idea was doomed. The underlings knew they were part of an inbred business structure.

They knew that they would shake the fallen executive's hand on the way out the door and get ready for his or her replacement, ready to do it again and again until they retired or got fired themselves.

As an example, I had a client who owned a large manufacturing company in the San Fernando Valley, just outside of Los Angeles, that specialized in subcontract machine work. Another client I had helped to overcome some organizational and business difficulties referred him to me. As I sat across from the man, who was in his mid-forties, he told me that he had lost several large accounts that he had worked with for over ten years. Without notice they pulled several large jobs in progress, as well as several promised future projects. He didn't have a clue as to the reason why this happened because the customers were all avoiding him. Prior to my arrival, he had been given advice from another consulting company to reduce overhead and payroll so as to streamline the business operation and optimize profits. They advised him to do this during a period of time when business was booming and profitable and in the interest of efficiency and increased profits, he happily complied.

During my initial interview with him, we were interrupted by several important phone calls relating to the liquidation of his luxury cars and vacation homes, as well as other personal assets. Needless to say, he was not a happy camper.

As I mentioned earlier, part of my plan of attack in these situations was to interview each employee in order to gain their perspective. This required at least twenty minutes of individual interview time. Since there were over 150 employees, it took a while to figure out how and why the wheels had come off of this profitable business. During this process, I spoke to everyone, from top management to the janitor, asking the same questions of each one. When I was done, I prepared a report for the owner. I outlined the key problems that existed and was able to point to one instance that may have triggered the whole business downturn.

It seems that the consulting company that advised the business owner to make the cutbacks did an analysis of each department and recommended the firing of people who were not deemed essential to the overall business structure. One of those people was a fellow who worked in the tool crib and earned the princely sum of $10.00 per hour. This man would sharpen all of the bits and cutting tools needed for each job, get the blueprints required for that job, and put everything in a plastic bag. As each machine operator finished a job, they would return the bits and plans from the completed job and pick up the set needed for the next job. The previous consulting firm deemed his job, along with others in different departments, as inefficient. They suggested that they be eliminated because the machine operators should be able to sharpen their own bits and tools and get their own blueprints. On the surface, this seemed to make sense. In reality, the machine operators were better at running their machines than they were sharpening bits and tools. The sharpening area became a meeting place for all of the employees waiting to use the grinders and, instead of producing parts, they were constantly looking for blueprints that always seemed to be misplaced. I was able to determine all of this by doing the employee interviews. The clearest view to the source of the problem came from one employee. This employee had been with the company since its inception and had maintained the same position as a maintenance man for over thirty years. I remember that he was almost the last person to be interviewed. In the previous employee interviews, I got a picture of inefficiency and production loss but no one could put their finger on the cause or how to remedy it. In response to simple operational questions, the maintenance worker gave me his perspective on what had gone wrong. I then went to several key people, all of whom I had previously interviewed, and put together a time line as to when the problem started. I did a time motion study concerning the current situation of tool sharpening and general production utilization. It seemed that the maintenance man was right. I wrote my report and sat across the desk from the owner as he read it.

If I were writing a work of fiction, I would tell you that the owner stood up after reading my report, shook my hand, gave the long time employee with the special insight a raise and then moved forward to implement the necessary production changes. The reality was that he looked at me with a red face and exasperated look and called in several key people to ask if they concurred with my analysis. When they answered affirmatively, he asked me for a final billing statement and to my amazement, told me that my services were no longer needed. I heard through the grapevine that he said he felt foolish at that moment and that he was angry that the reason for a large part of the organizational failure came from such a simple source. I can honestly say that this incident really got me thinking about my future as a business consultant. It made me think of the old saying, "No good deed goes unpunished". The only difference between this man and the rest of us is the degree of trust we have for simple advice and how we make ourselves available to receive it. The fellow who gave me the insight was a person who had a lot invested from a time standpoint and wanted the business to succeed as much as the owner. The problem was that until I sat down to interview him he had no chance to share his perspective.

The second lesson to be learned in this chapter of John concerns relaxation and taking well-deserved time off. I believe that God recorded everything that is written in the bible for the purpose of teaching and example. In this chapter it says that after the wedding in Cana, Jesus went to Capernaum for a few days with his mother and His disciples. In my imagination I can hear the questions from the apostles, "Turning water into wine, that was cool. Can you teach us how to do that?" or "What happened back there? Tell me again how you did that and why you did that?" The journey must have been full of good conversation like that while Jesus probably gave them answers to their questions.

Capernaum is located on the North West shore of the Sea of Galilee and in the time of Jesus was a fishing village of 1,000 to

1,500 people. It was a place of familiarity to the first apostles and I'm sure a place where they all felt comfortable. It is thought that Peter married a woman from Capernaum and that the ruins of his home exist there today. One of the great things about having faith in who Jesus was and is, is that there are historical references to places like Capernaum. The town is a physical and historical testament to Christ living as a man and performing miracles as God. After being rejected in Nazareth, Jesus based His ministry in Capernaum and there are numerous mentions of the town in the New Testament.

Back to the business reference in this part of John, the lesson is simple. Take the time to get to know those who are with you in the good fight. Break bread, relax and discuss what is going on in the business or organization. It is almost impossible to not care about a person or organization that cares about you. Current business practices may not encourage this type of activity between management and employees because of a fear that familiarity may not be a good thing, but as a believer in Jesus Christ, I believe that this biblical example calls us to make the effort.

Lastly, in the second chapter it says that Jesus went to the temple at Passover and watched as the business people went about their daily transactions. The bible says that these people were engaged in the selling of sacrificial animals to the pilgrims who came to the temple to worship. In the past, I have always thought of this incident as being just a spontaneous response to a situation that Jesus came upon randomly. I now believe that Jesus knew that the business people were taking advantage of their customers and were operating outside of the law of God. He probably put this whole incident on His "to do" list or daily planner. They were probably charging too much, misrepresenting their products and most likely, delivering an inferior product at an inflated price. In effect, they were being unfair and disingenuous in their business practices by acting if they were helping their customers, when in fact they were gouging them.

The bible then says that Jesus braided a whip as He watched all of this business chicanery unfold in front of Him. I can only imagine that the business people were far too engaged in the money transactions to pay proper attention to Jesus in the corner doing His braiding. They might have had a tinge of guilt as they proceeded to do something they knew to be immoral in front of the rabbi that they saw out of the corner of their eye. But they never expected Him to come over and drive them and their animals from the temple, flip over their merchandise tables and scatter their hard earned money all over the floor. No, that was the last thing they expected, because they had gotten away with it for so long that it became an expected way of doing business.

I believe that God outlines things and events in the bible for a purpose so that we may have a clue as to how to act in our daily business and personal lives. Let's take a look at some modern day examples that may be of the same caliber of offensive business practices that Jesus would view as comparable to the biblical example. Using the same false guidelines of the moneychangers in the temple, we will look at business and organizational entities that represent themselves to be compassionate to the poor and disadvantaged when in fact they are predatory and lack any compassion for their clients. They are driven by profit and the ability to take advantage of a person down on their luck. After the transaction, that person is worse off, financially and/or emotionally.

Abortion Clinics

Don't let anyone tell you differently, these entities exist because of their motive to make a profit. There is big money to be made in the business of killing the unborn. That market will only continue to expand as the scientific community sees the potential uses for the fetus in the area of stem cell research. If the abortion industry gets their way, we will see their clinics operate like seedy collection businesses that pay for blood and plasma. People will be encouraged to continue to act immorally and "sell" their fetus in the future. It doesn't matter if the abortion clinic is privately owned by a doctor or by a so-called non-profit organization. No matter how much they claim to help the poor or how much they say they are interested in the rights of women, they are making a lot of "misery" money, a good portion of it coming from our tax dollars.

Payday Loan Offices

Let's see, how can we make a person, who already demonstrates an inability to handle their personal finances, worse off in the quickest possible manner? I know, let's set up a business that will loan small amounts of money at extreme interest rates that will, at best, help that person avoid the inevitable for one or two days and complete their ruinous financial slide. In the 1920's, gangsters called this "loan sharking", a lending practice that was designed to capture some poor soul in a net that he or she could not escape. If they did run away, the lender would take out their kneecap for extra interest.

As an example, several years ago, when this type of business was allowed to operate in California, they said that their business purpose was to provide a lending source to the poor and disenfranchised. This should always be a red flag when someone tells you that they are doing whatever they are doing because they want to help the poor and downtrodden. This goes for phony preachers, charlatans and other liars who really want to prey on the very ones they claim to want to help (see previous example).

According to the lobbyists who promoted this business idea to the California legislators said that payday loans were only used for emergencies and for a short time period. The opposite appears to have occurred, as the average customer makes eleven transactions per year and a majority of those transactions are made to cover a previous loan.

Payday loans are usually small, short-term loans made at extremely high interest rates. Typically, a borrower writes a personal check for $100-$300, plus a fee, payable to the lender. The lender agrees to hold on to the check until the borrower's next payday, usually one week to one month later, and only then will the check be deposited. In return, the borrower gets cash immediately. The fees for payday loans are extremely high; up to $17.50 for every $100 borrowed, up to a maximum of $300. The interest rates for such transactions are staggering; 911% for a one-week loan, 456% for a two-week loan and 212% for a one-month loan.

Stories from payday loan customers make the results of these burdensome loans clear. Consumers take them to meet an immediate need, find themselves unable to meet their needs on their next payday, take subsequent loans and quickly get trapped by the outlandish fees. Payday lenders claim they are the only option for debt-strapped consumers. But borrowing more money at triple-digit interest rates is never the right solution for people in debt. Instead, payday loans make problems worse. As the data shows, virtually everyone takes more than one payday loan and thus the loans are similar to an addiction. This is not a legitimate loan product that benefits consumers. In fact, because most consumers believe they could be prosecuted for passing a bad check, the payday loan suddenly becomes their priority debt. Thus, the original debt problems that brought them to the lender often cannot be resolved.

The last point I will make regarding this type of business comes from The Center for Responsible Lending. This organization states that it is estimated that predatory lending costs American consumers $3.4 billion per year in excess fees. The payday lending business model is designed to keep borrowers in chronic debt, not to provide one-time assistance during a financial emergency. In many ways, **military personnel are ideal targets for these abusive payday loans.** They have a steady income from the government; they are struggling to support a family on that income; and above all, they are honest and will work hard to repay the loan. With new recruits making an average of $1,200 per month, it is easy to see how the lure of "quick" and "easy" cash captures the interest - and then the hard-earned wages - of military personnel. The only difference between the gangster's way and today is that you get to keep your kneecaps, for now anyway.

Rent-To-Own Furniture

Rent-to-own furniture companies have been the subject of considerable scrutiny recently. Although not every rent-to-own company merits suspicion, consumers are well advised to be wary. In some cases, consumers could end up paying as much as 50 percent more than the retail price for an item purchased through lease or rent-to-buy plans. Many furniture rental companies require that an item be leased for a minimum of one or two years before it may be purchased.

Again, the refrain from this industry is that they help people who are poor and unable to buy furniture because of their financial or credit circumstances. There are many furniture rental companies who run an ethical business with rentals to businesses and individuals who understand that the increased cost is related to convenience or that it can be written off. By the same token, there are many rental companies that are simply stealing from their disadvantaged customers.

In addition to these examples you could add in pawn shops, get rich quick schemes that involve the buying of foreclosed homes, bars, big hotel chains that derive a portion of their income from the sale of in room pornography, strip clubs, porn shops, etc.

As Christians, we should not be involved in any business related to the promotion of misery or sinfulness of others. We should seek out the proprietors of these businesses and regard them to be part of our daily missionary effort. We are being hypocritical if we work for or own a business that is doing anything immoral.

In other words, we can't earn "misery money" and claim it comes from God.

Jesus said that He would be back. He will come this time to judge, not to be hung on a tree. The reason that we have businesses operating outside of God's law is because they don't think that God is paying attention and that they will get away with their immoral deeds without consequence.

The second chapter of John tells us differently.

The following are a few suggestions on how we can make a difference in our Christian business walk. If you think about it, you will come up with many more effective ways to turn the business community back to God.

1. If you use a form of advertising such as newspapers, classified phone books, radio, television or the Internet, take a hard look at what else it is that they are selling. As a Christian businessperson, you are given the freedom to not advertise with an ungodly company. If they promote immoral behavior, don't advertise with them. This is particularly effective when you write a letter to their management telling them the reason you won't give them anymore of your money. If enough businesspeople refuse to support advertising venues that promote strip clubs, filthy movies, entertainment and other contributors to the moral breakdown of our society, they will pay attention. If you think about it, there are very few advertising venues that do not have some sort of moral and sinful tainting.

2. Don't spend money to stay in a hotel or a motel that derives part of its income from the sale of pornography. It is surprising how many large hotel and motel operators are in league with the pornography industry. When revenue from this source is listed in an earnings report, it is always denoted

as something like "multimedia entertainment income" or something like that. If it wasn't shameful income, the accountants would list is as "dirty movie money" or "XXX porn income". I guarantee you that those headings will never be listed in an annual report.

3. Tell your local and long distance phone companies that you are going to find an alternative to their services if they continue to offer phone sex related services.

4. Contact your politicians on a regular basis and let them know that you are willing to support them if they promote a Godly agenda and that you will help to defeat them if they do not.

5. Quit supporting ungodly entertainment. This applies to theaters, music, publications, television and the Internet. Stop giving them money to produce more.

Notes

Notes

Chapter Three

$\mathcal{C}$hapter three opens with Jesus speaking to Nicodemus, a respected religious leader. The bible tells us that Nicodemus met with Jesus after dark, indicating that what he wanted to talk about was something that he wanted to keep on the hush-hush, if you get my drift. In that meeting, Jesus laid down some absolutes of faith that surprised the Pharisee and undoubtedly changed his perspective on who Jesus was.

Chapter three goes on to tell us how Jesus and His disciples stayed in Judea and baptized believers across the river from John the Baptist and his followers. A competition started to develop between both camps when rumors started that Jesus and His apostles were taking business away from John the Baptist and his crew. John the Baptist settled the problem before it got started and explained that both parties were on the same team and that the focus should be on the bigger picture, not on negative competitive details. In this example, he explains to his team that Jesus is the Messiah and their job is to submit to His authority and work along side Jesus and His disciples.

Chapter Three Business Lesson

Several years ago, I received a phone call from a lady whom I had met years before. She was a prominent member of our community and the purpose of her call was to tell me that I had been nominated to become a board member of a local charity. The charitable organization had, and still has, a terrific reputation for helping those in our community who are in need of food, clothing and shelter. The board members are all people who are active in various charitable and social organizations in our community and seem to be genuinely sincere in their desire to help the less fortunate. After being elected to the board, I spent the next year working on various committees that were all designed to facilitate the charitable goals of the organization. In joining the board, I made a false assumption. I assumed that because they were doing such good things for their fellow man, that they must know who Christ is. When I mentioned that I attended a bible-based church, my fellow board members looked at me like I had two heads. When I suggested that we pray before a committee meeting, the reaction was less than positive. I slowly came to the conclusion that this was an organization that is designed to glorify man and not God.

Nicodemus was a man who fed and clothed the poor and was a great leader in his church. He did these things (I am sure) for the same reasons that many charitable organizations do, they just believe that doing good will somehow make everything balance out. As Jesus explained to Nicodemus, salvation comes from knowing and believing that He is the Son of God and through that belief, we are saved. I can tell you that there were other Christians on the board and they did not let their faith go before them. It is sad to say that like myself, they never addressed the issue openly of how we should praise God for His works through the organization and how much more success the organization would have if we did. The fact is that we didn't want to be considered pushy and rude or be considered a "religious fanatic" when in fact the third chapter of John calls us to be just that, by declaring just who Jesus Christ is. As I said in the beginning, we will go and send others to the ends of the earth to share the word of Jesus Christ but will pass by an organization or business that is "doing good" but does not know who Jesus is. I wish that I could tell you that I made some great stand for Christ in this case, but sadly cannot; I resigned from the board and abandoned an opportunity to be a business missionary, a mistake I will not make again if the opportunity presents itself.

In the second part of chapter three, we get a glimpse of the leadership capabilities of John the Baptist. When faced with rumor and potentially derisive attitudes among his organization, John went to the root of his faith that Jesus was the redeemer and stopped the revolt before it got started.

In 1968, I joined the United States Marine Corps. I remember the words that the recruiter said that made me want to sign up. He promised that if I was wounded or died on the field of battle, that my fellow marines would not leave me there. Conversely, I understood that my obligation was to do the same for them. Arriving in San Diego for my basic training, feeling assured that I was joining an outfit that lived by such lofty goals; I was greeted by the reality that what I had really signed up for was hell on earth for thirteen weeks.

Having grown up in Southern California in the fifties and sixties, I was never exposed to racism or racial hatred until I arrived at boot camp. I had heard smear words from different adults growing up but I never made the connection that you should hate someone for the color of their skin until then. The idea of basic training was, and still is, to break the recruit down and then build them back up so that they become an effective soldier. Our drill instructors did their jobs with a level of unmatched enthusiasm. I did what they wanted just so that I could get out of there by graduating with my platoon and not be held back. I heard the drill instructors call out racial slurs that I had never heard before or since that time.

It was a surreal experience, flying to the war on a Continental airlines jet, with stewardesses no less. When I arrived in Okinawa for staging, I was introduced to the real world of the Marine Corps of the 1960's, which dictated that you were to hang out with those of your own race and no one else. This was amplified when I arrived at my final base located outside of Da Nang, Viet Nam. While I was stationed at Red Beach, as part of the third Marine Amphibious Brigade, I learned that if you wanted to take a shower, it was necessary to have a marine of your own ethnicity stand at the door to guard you so that another marine wouldn't try to kill or maim you. As absurd as it may seem, marines were killing and injuring each other by rolling live grenades into showers or bathrooms, all because of the simmering racial feud that was taking place. This practice was, and still is, called "fragging". People who were on the same team, so to speak, were poisoned by some bad leadership and allowed to destroy each other.

After one month of this life, I volunteered for the Combined Action Program, which was a field operation located thirty-five miles from Da Nang. Because we were a smaller unit and we were more dependent on each other, our chances of dying or getting hurt came from the enemy outside of our camp and not from within.

There is an old Sicilian saying, "A fish stinks from the head first". I have always taken this to mean that if there are problems in an organization, it comes first from leadership. The drill instructors of the Viet Nam era were given the inspiration to manage people the way they did from those above them. To be fair, racial feelings of injustice and anger were alive and well in this period of American history and it didn't seem to take much to get people upset. As I look back on that era, I am really amazed that we survived as a country and as a society because of the amount of anger and unhappiness that existed. So much for the "Free Love" and "Age of Aquarius" period, known as the 1960's.

John the Baptist excelled as a leader because he eliminated feelings of separation among his followers before it could start. He didn't allow anyone to build a divide between his followers and the followers of Jesus. He recognized that to be successful in their mission, there could be no lack of teamwork.

A major problem in business is the lack of management direction between employees, groups, divisions, regions, etc. We constantly allow and overlook strife between the night shift and the day shift, the weekend crew and the weekday crew etc... God calls us to promote harmony in the work place and create a work environment that encourages employees and management to get along and be productive.

The bright side to my story is that I believe that the Marines have changed the way that they manage and motivate their troops and that the divided management approach is no longer practiced. The reason I know this is by talking to young marines who have recently gone through boot camp, reading articles about how they are trained and watching how heroically they are operating in the various war zones going on around the world. Good leadership allows those being led to concentrate on their mission and performance, not worrying about the true motivation of their leadership. I believe another reason that this does not exist to the degree that it did is because we have a volunteer military and everyone who is part of it is there because they want to be.

The casual observer of any organization can easily identify good leadership and bad leadership. Jealousy and infighting can stop everyone from accomplishing their set of common goals. A great manager will find contentment in their job. He or she will not undermine the authority of the owner and will improve as a manager by serving those that they manage.

Questions:

1. Are there conflicts between shifts, crews or divisions in your business or organization?

2. Do different departments stand up for each other? As an example, does the sales staff defend the production staff to the customer? Does the new employee in the production area hear good things about sales and office staff during the first few days of employment?

3. How does the owner or manager speak about their staff ?

Notes

Chapter Four

*C*hapter four opens with the words of Jesus. It was becoming apparent to many who He was and the Pharisees were getting concerned because Jesus and His apostles were gaining many converts. Jesus leaves his disciples to baptize the new converts and headed back to Galilee from Judea.

On His way, He runs into a Samaritan woman and has an interesting conversation with her at Jacob's well. Much to the puzzlement of those apostles who traveled with Him, Jesus was eventually engaged by the whole village and decided to stay for a couple of days.

Jesus went back to Galilee and the townspeople's previous reactions caused Him to lament that a prophet was honored everywhere, except in his hometown. This time they welcomed Him back. He was now a celebrity because of the miracles they saw Him perform over the Passover holiday in Jerusalem. During this visit, a government official asked Jesus to heal his son, and when Jesus did, the man's entire household became believers in Jesus.

Chapter Four Business Lesson

In chapter four, Jesus lays out a basic point of business and organizational success. He delegated authority to his management staff and had them perform the daily tasks of baptizing new believers while He went on the road to work on new market development. Jesus could have stayed and baptized the many new followers and converts but He knew that if He did, He would limit the growth of the church organization.

I would like to point out several different situations that business people find themselves in quite frequently. In the first situation, the owner or manager is very interested in maintaining control and has no confidence in anyone else to do things right. In the second, a distrustful owner or manager can't let go because he or she is afraid that others can't be trusted with authority. There can be other reasons to keep a tight grip on your business or organization, but these two examples seem to be most prevalent. In these cases, the owners and managers develop a very high opinion of themselves and their capabilities. They tend to bluster and position themselves as being irreplaceable, much like the rudder of a ship or the straw that stirs the drink. There are other reasons that owners or managers will not share duties, and most are based on insecurities, false assumptions and unrealistic expectations of themselves and others.

In order to better illustrate this situation, let's look at a historical example involving the naval exploits of Germany and England, dating from the 1920's into the 1940's.

As a ruler of the seas, England found itself in a state of decline early in the twentieth century. Falling behind as a naval power to other European countries and the United States, the British designed and built a new breed of warship known as the Admiral class. Because of treaty limitations regarding the size and tonnage of warships, the British navy built only one of these sea-going monsters. The HMS Hood was quite a sight to see, as she was regarded as the fastest battleship of her size (top speed around 32 knots) and on her massive bow, fifteen inch guns were positioned to destroy an enemy or protect a friend. It should be noted that the Hood was the longest ship of its kind in the world.

The Hood was a floating example of the power of the Royal navy and spent most of her time sailing to ports of call simply "showing the flag". This act was designed to awe, impress, dominate and terrify potential and real enemies and to bring comfort to England's friends. When this ship came to visit, people paid attention.

After World War One, Germany was bound by the Versailles treaty and was limited in regards to the size of their naval warships. Hitler flaunted the treaty and went about to build two "F" class ships, the Bismarck (named after German Chancellor Otto Von Bismarck) and the Tirpitz. Launched on February 14, 1939, the 51,000 ton symbol of German naval domination was made ready for her date with history. Like her English counterpart, the Bismarck was considered to be more of a symbol than a weapon and both of these floating monstrosities were considered to be unsinkable.

On the twenty first of May, 1941, the Hood, accompanied by a smaller naval ship, The Prince of Wales, met the Bismarck, escorted by the Prinz Eugen, on a watery Atlantic Ocean battlefield. In less than five salvos from the Bismarck, the Hood took an unfortunate shot to its magazine section and promptly broke in two, sinking to the bottom with 1600 plus sailors. The Bismarck took direct hits to its bridge and bow with little to show for it but did sustain rudder and propeller damage, making it able to move only in a very tight circle, not a very evasive movement for a large ship. The Prince of Wales escaped in the fog and was able to track the German ships until help could arrive. The English ships fired upon the wounded ship and within 72 hours after the sinking of the Hood, the Bismarck went down with over 2000 sailors aboard.

Those German sailors who were fished out of the sea by their English counterparts were pleasantly surprised by the treatment they received. Many of them reported that the great Bismarck was actually scuttled by its captain and crew, rather than face capture.

On a final and ironic note, the Hood was sunk on an English

national day of pride known as Empire day. Any celebration that Hitler may have felt like doing was certainly measured when he found out that the pride of the Third Reich was resting on the bottom of the Atlantic with the mighty symbol of power belonging to the English navy.

It doesn't matter how much we bluster and make ourselves to appear invincible, if we think that we, or our organization, is unsinkable and nothing can happen to stop future success, just imagine if you, the captain, gets hurt or incapacitated. If we don't spread the trust and responsibilities to others and we insist on doing everything ourselves, "our way", we will sink the organization quickly - even if we only receive damage to a small and insignificant area of our "ship", like the rudder.

Christ knew that He would not be with His management team forever and I am sure that they made plenty of mistakes while they were learning. The key to His ministry organization was how those apostles managed when He was gone. If you look at the apostles' actions and behavior when Jesus was with them, they didn't always look like they were the right choices to accomplish God's ambitious organizational plan. When Jesus was abducted, the whole organization appeared to come apart. They were even to the point of denying, and some did deny, who they were and who Jesus was. It wasn't until Christ rose from the dead that they truly understood who He was and what their management role would be and they pursued it without reserve. The fact is that each one of them was tortured and (with the exception of John) died lonely and painful deaths at the hands of their enemies. All any of them would have had to say was, "it was just a joke, we made it up", but they didn't, and because they were prepared, they accomplished their objective.

While His disciples were on a lunch run in town, Jesus spoke to the woman at Jacob's well. If I lived during this historical period (and I am grateful to God that I didn't) and I had a choice between being a man or a woman, it would have been an easy choice.

Women did not have equal standing with men during this time period and Christ continually placed women at pivotal points of progress in His ministry. The business lesson from this part of the chapter is to broaden your potential marketplace, speak to anyone who has an interest, be "on message" with everyone that you meet and have a clear mission statement. Above all, be prepared to be flexible and able to handle the success that may come of your efforts. In the example that Jesus gives us, He changed His schedule and stuck around a few extra days to handle the new business that was generated.

Jesus spoke to this woman, who was a social outcast from her own town, and recognized that she had the potential to influence everyone in her community. He was right, because in the end, she brought the whole town to Jesus The bible tells us that even though she was socially suspect, the woman had some credibility and the people came to hear Jesus speak because of her.

Many times, a business or an organization will be able to get the attention of potential customers or members and fail to deliver a clear and concise message. In this example, however, Jesus shows that He knew how get the attention of others and then deliver His message in a succinct manner so that, as the bible tells us, the people of the town believed.

The last part of this chapter addresses a common human shortcoming, lack of vision. We see things the way we want to see them, not as they are. The people of Galilee saw Jesus as the son of Joseph and Mary and could not accept Him as the Son of God. In this chapter, they did seem to move toward the realization of who He was but seem to be drawn more to His celebrity and fame that came as a result of the miracles that He performed.

In business, I have been amazed by the lack of vision of others and their unwillingness to accept new ideas. If you want to know the true depths of frustration, just introduce a new service or product to people and it seems that they will do everything that they can to avoid using it. As an example, I have been amazed at how many owners and managers refuse to use computers or other new technology in their business or organization or to maximize the use of business related software.

As an example of this, go back with me to the invention of Scotch tape. 3M Corporation introduced Scotch tape way back in the 1920's. The inventor, Richard Drew, was an engineer for the Minnesota based company and during the testing of sand paper products in an auto body repair shop, and saw a need for an adhesive that would hold paper on the fender so that the painter could separate two colors of paint evenly. The marketing and sales people at 3M saw the potential business applications for the transparent adhesive and set out to convince business owners and managers that they had a great product that would make their business life better. There was only one problem. Up until then, business people used string to bundle everything from paper to rags and really didn't see much value in switching to the new product. There was a whole business infrastructure that sold and marketed string in varying lengths, quantity, quality and price. There was a whole customer base that bundled their paper documents and records with string and, true to their human nature, they were resistant to making any sort of change. As hard as it is to imagine a world without scotch tape, in reality it took a great deal of marketing and sales perseverance to get people to buy it.

In my own life, I have missed many financial, career and personal opportunities because I just couldn't see the obvious potential. I am sorry to say that if I was a citizen of Galilee during this period of time, I might have missed who Jesus was and is. Man, by nature, can resist change and overlook the obvious.

Based on the contents of Chapter Four, the following questions may be asked about any business or organization.

Questions:

1. What would happen to your business or organization if you were to die or become disabled?

2. Have you prepared for a successor if something should happen to you?

3. Have you evaluated everyone in your organization or business from the standpoint of future leadership? potential? Have you let them know what that role will be?

4. Does the organization or business limit its potential marketplace by pre-disqualifying their customer base on the basis of race, age, sex, social or financial prejudice?

5. When the business or organization gets an opportunity to speak before a potential customer or membership base is it "on message" and are you able to share base values and mission goals in a clear and concise manner?

6. When the organization or business does speak to potential customers or members, do they respond favorably by buying what you are selling? Why?

Notes

Chapter Five

*C*hapter five begins with Jesus returning to Jerusalem for one of the Jewish holy days. In the course of that journey, He encounters a man who has been sick for thirty-eight years. Jesus asks the man, "Would you like to get well?" The man answers that every time he tries to get to the healing waters at the pool of Bethesda, others who arrive ahead of him block him. Jesus tells the man to pick up his mat and walk, which he does immediately.

After the man is healed, he tells everyone, including the religious leaders of the day who have tried to prosecute Jesus for breaking the law by healing on the Sabbath. Later in this chapter, He gives an example of the importance of using third party testimony to promote your cause and ideas. Jesus used John the Baptist, God the Father and Holy Scripture to make His point. He basically said, "If you don't believe me, believe those who give testimony of me".

Chapter Five Business Lesson

As a Christian business or organization leader, we are required to help those people we meet on our journey through life. The example that Christ gives us is one that can be emulated daily in our business life. We will run across many who will be in need of a job and will expect you and others to pick them up and carry them to success. In this example Jesus gave the man an opportunity to get up by himself and be healed. The man, like many of us, had good excuses as to why he failed to get to the water for all those years but on this day, he took the help that was offered and he was healed. Jesus didn't swoop him up in His arms and carry him to the water, He simply gave the crippled man the opportunity for healing and it was up to the man to accept the help. As business people, we are called to offer help to others in the way of jobs and other opportunities. It is up to the recipient to receive or deny that opportunity.

I submit to you an example of a man who used this biblical example as a blueprint for his business success. In an era that was dominated by conflict between workers and management, union strikes, management lockouts and general conditions of war between the classes, Henry Heinz was a Godly example of a person who lifted others up. He was truly one of the most successful business people in American history.

Henry J. Heinz was born in 1844, on the south side of what is now the city of Pittsburgh, Pennsylvania. His parents were first generation immigrants of Bavaria and Germany. The garden was a central point in their family life. Henry not only learned how to grow vegetables from his parents, He also learned Christian values that guided him his entire life. From these humble beginnings, Henry started to sell bottles of horseradish, first to neighbors and then to local stores, truly starting as a home business. Throughout his life, Heinz met all of the challenges of a business with a Godly heart. While he attained worldly success and was able to match the accomplishments of Rockefeller and Carnegie from a business point of view, he was without a doubt considered a great success in God's eyes because of his accomplishments in faith.

Henry Heinz lived by two memorable sayings. One was that he felt that every business must be "run by heart power" and the other was, "Make all you can honestly, save all you can prudently, give all you can wisely". In 1901, Henry Heinz visited Japan and was inspired to start an organized Sunday school program there. He spent the rest of his life nurturing this Christian program not only in Japan, but also in China, Korea, Russia and here at home in the US.

It is possible and probable that his missionary efforts planted the seeds of faith in Asia and is at least partly responsible for the success of the church that, although still persecuted in some of these places, has grown despite the oppression.

Henry Heinz donated great sums of money to his community. He started insurance companies, banks and other great financial institutions. He supported all sorts of children's organizations and charities, had buildings named after him and was invited to sit on the board of directors for many prestigious business and charitable organizations. During his management tenure, Henry Heinz was most proud of the fact that his company never had a labor dispute with its employees. This was an amazing accomplishment because of the era. Some of the greatest labor unrest in American business history took place at this time. Many business leaders and union organizations provoked strife between companies and workers through this period of American business history.

In John 4 verses 1-3, Jesus gives us an example of delegating authority. Henry Heinz lived this example by creating a management environment that nurtured young employees in the belief that there was a future for them with his company. In accordance with John 3:27-36, he encouraged his managers to find contentment in their job and to encourage as well as serve others. His management team did not undermine the authority of those above them and worked very hard to let employees know that upper management valued their service. Henry Heinz subscribed to the belief that if employers stayed in close, sympathetic touch with their employees, the most serious labor disputes would melt away and that all that remained would be settled in friendship and amity. On a regular basis, meetings were held in which employees could engage in friendly discussion with management, exchanging ideas designed to enrich the company. Without prompting or complaining, the employees worked in a business environment that was designed to bring comfort to them while they were there. Mr. Heinz built lecture halls, libraries, dining areas and bathrooms (a real employee perk at that time), lunchrooms and a roof garden for their use. He also brought in multiple works of art and historical pictures, filled the libraries with classic books and provided regular entertainment from the best vaudeville and minstrel acts of the day. When he was asked late in his life to evaluate his greatest business success, he said he was most pleased that his employees never felt the need to go on strike or have a labor dispute.

Henry Heinz was a Godly man who attained much and was blessed in every part of his life. In faith he faced financial hardships, the loss of loved ones and the challenges and trappings of success. Of all his legacies, the ones in faith are the most substantial and ongoing. He wasn't a pushover; while he gave much to his employees, he expected much from them in return. Through his Christian faith, he gave others an opportunity to improve their situation in life and achieve great personal success.

In the latter part of this chapter, we find that Jesus makes use of "third party testimony" to sustain His point to His critics. This testimony was viable because the religious leaders had already scrutinized John the Baptist, and they certainly knew the word of God. Both of these parties gave strong testimony as to who Jesus was and is.

I have found it very beneficial in my business life to have this sort of third party testimony available for potential clients, as it is a very effective way to develop new business. Some of the strongest business leads you can possibly have are those referrals from an existing satisfied customer or client. If we will treat customers and employees as Jesus treated the crippled man in this chapter, they will appreciate our efforts, making sure that our reputation travels before us.

Questions:

1. In your business or organization, do workers feel that they have the support of ownership and management to grow in their positions?

2. Do management and ownership look down on workers, see them as equals or fear them?

3. Is your business or organization worthy of good, third party references and do you receive them?

Notes

Chapter Six

I love chapter six because it is a great learning tool for teaching management by committee. As Jesus and His disciples were traveling and teaching, they were followed by huge crowds of people who wanted to hear what Jesus had to say. At one point, Jesus asked Philip if he had any ideas on how to feed the multitude of followers that had gathered with them in the middle of nowhere. Philip's response was that it would cost a fortune and there were no supplies available where they were, geographically. Another apostle spoke up and tried his best to at least give some type of positive response and said that there was a young boy in the crowd who had two fish and five barley loaves, not that it would do much good.

Jesus told them to have everyone in the crowd sit down. He then blessed the food that the young boy had with him and had His disciples pass it out to those who had gathered on the grassy slopes. After everyone had eaten, He had the disciples collect all of the leftovers so that nothing was wasted. They collected twelve baskets of food that hadn't been eaten. The response of the crowd was so great that Jesus had to flee into the hills to avoid the appreciative crowd that had witnessed the miracle.

The chapter then talks of the time the apostles saw Jesus walking on water and how the crowds followed Him just so they could see the next miracle. When Jesus told the crowds who He was and why He came, the bible says that many disciples turned away and deserted

Him. The ones that stayed with Him declared their faith in Him and promised to stick with Him to the end.

Chapter Six Business Lesson

When Jesus asked His disciples to come up with a plan of action, I'm sure that he was testing them to see who had been paying attention. While I'm not saying that I would have done any better, the apostles had been in the presence of Jesus on a daily basis up to that point and had seen miracles performed daily. From healing friends and strangers, to turning water into wine, to bringing prophetic words to life and fulfilling them. A case could be made that these people had the very best view of the wonders of Jesus' ministry. Despite their special opportunity for insight, not one of them took the leap of faith required to solve the daunting logistical problem at hand. Jesus showed patience by directing that the small amount of bread and fish be collected and blessed. Without a doubt, the apostles would learn from this example and make the correct management decisions in the future. In business situations, we are faced with overwhelming daily problems that include meeting payroll, collecting money and making customers and employees happy, as well as monumental crisis moments that must be dealt with. Just as He asked the apostles, God asks us what we are going to do when we are faced with an impossible situation or problem? The simplest answer can be the most difficult. Despite our failure to do the right thing the first time, we are sometimes given another opportunity to operate in faith.

The following is an example of how business, intentionally or not, followed God's word and overcame a problem that, if handled in another way, could have destroyed the company.

The Johnson and Johnson Company distributes an over the counter analgesic medicine called Tylenol. In 1982, this product had a 35% share of the American market and those sales represented 15% of the entire company's profits. Out of nowhere, Johnson and

Johnson was faced with their product supply being contaminated with cyanide, causing great panic in the buying public since seven deaths were attributed to the contamination

This problem really seemed to blind side the company and it caused a great deal of confusion as to how they should react. As a result, Johnson and Johnson suffered a one billion dollar loss and devaluation as a result of their reaction to this unfortunate event.

In 1986, another act of tampering occurred. This time the company took decisive steps to correct the situation, showing that they had learned from the previous incident. They acted quickly to remove all of the Tylenol inventory from the shelves, nationwide. They also made a commitment to their customer base that they would not restock with new product until proper changes were made to the product's packaging in order to prevent further possible contamination or tampering. The end result of this decisive strategy was the development of tamper proof packaging designed to curtail future incidents and to restore the faith of consumers in the safety of the product. In fact, the customer base grew, as the buying public seemed to show their appreciation for how Johnson and Johnson reacted to the challenge.

When Jesus posed the question regarding the feeding of the crowd of followers, I'm positive that each of the apostles knew the answer to His question. Even though the course of action was evident, they hesitated. After Jesus performed the miracle of the loaves and fishes, they were reinforced in their faith and in the future called on that faith so as to allow God to perform miracles through them. Without the testing and failure to react, the apostles could not grow into being the leaders that they eventually became. In business, we face the same challenges to our faith in our daily duties and the choice to react in the correct and moral way is always daunting. There have been other companies that have faced acts of product sabotage and failed to meet the problem in a moral and honest way. They suffered in the marketplace and some never recovered.

Every business or organization reaches the point that the owner or founder can no longer do all of the planning and leading. In this example, Jesus knew that the apostles were not ready to run things just yet and, as you can see, it caused His followers to broaden their perspective. Examples of how others make mistakes and more importantly, correct their mistakes, gives us the courage to take that step of faith and make faithful business and organizational decisions. I have seen good businesses stifled and unable to go to the next level because the owner didn't want to go through this important management growth step.

The second point of this chapter pertains to losing good people for a variety of different reasons. For the benefit of the business or organization, people who have a hard time believing the core values presented by leadership should leave as soon as the situation becomes apparent. It is a business and organizational fact: At some point in time, you will lose good people; those who remain will become your loyal core. In the case of the Christian church, God used the apostles to help establish it among their Jewish base, but brought in a uniquely qualified outsider, Paul, to expand the market to the gentile world.

There is an old saying, "The graveyard is filled with irreplaceable people." In business, we have to be prepared to lose good people and ready to accept more good people who will replace them. We also need to appreciate those employees who stay through thick and thin and don't require a "miracle" every day or every moment of their working life. These are the people who share your core values and gain fulfillment through the sharing of those values.

In the early part of the 1990's, I had the great opportunity to visit a large aviation event that is held every summer in the Midwest part of the country. At that event, I was able to attend a lecture that featured the remaining crewmembers of Jimmy Doolittle's "Tokyo Raiders". For those of you who do not know who these men are and what they did, shame on you and your history teacher. Their example of following their leader because of shared values and mission achievement is one that should be a blueprint for any business leadership program.

When Japan attacked the United States at Pearl Harbor, they did so with the knowledge that it would be impossible for the United States to retaliate on their own homeland soil. At the time, the Japanese knew that we didn't have a bomber that could make a flight of that distance, so they felt pretty good about their safety from our military. In fact, the Japanese hoped that after they destroyed our fleet, we would have no taste for war and they could claim the Hawaiian Islands as their spoils of war. The warlords in Japan promised the emperor that the Japanese people had nothing to fear from their new enemy. They went about with an acquisition plan to take over every piece of real estate between Tokyo and Honolulu with impunity. The warlords of Japan were correct in their evaluation of the performance restrictions of American aircraft. They just didn't know about the determination of the people who flew those aircraft.

On April 18, 1942, the USS Hornet set sail for a secret position 600 miles off of the Japanese coast. Positioned on the deck of the Navy's newest carrier were sixteen B-25 "Mitchell" mid-range bombers and eighty men, who operated in secrecy and faith, ready to fly them. Their leader, Lieutenant Colonel James H. Doolittle, was assigned the task of putting together flight crews of men to volunteer for what amounted to being a "suicide mission". The crewmembers were never told what they were going to do and operated in blind faith that their mission would in some way help the war effort. In fact, one of the crewmembers that spoke told of how he was given navigational coordinates to the bomb site and remarked to the captain of that flight that the B-25 didn't have the fuel capacity to reach the target and make a safe return. The answer that the captain gave him was, "I know that."

Because the Japanese spotted the ships, it was necessary to alter the schedule. The first plane to take off from the carrier was flown by Jimmy Doolittle. This was a daring act because, up until that moment, a B-25 had never taken off from an aircraft carrier. The military had organized takeoff practices from the ground and knew that the B-25 had the capability to take off in the required distance, but the act of taking off from a moving ship, heaving on rough seas, was another story. The crewmember that spoke said that Doolittle's bravery that day inspired each and every pilot and crewmember to accomplish their mission.

After taking off from the darkened ship, with no return plan in place, these brave men delivered their limited ordinance to several Japanese mainland targets. Although they inflicted minimal damage that day, the mere fact that they had invaded enemy air space at all threw the Japanese war plan out the window. It is believed that Japan made several planning and strategic blunders as a result of this limited bombing attack, which may have caused them to eventually lose the war

Fifteen planes with seventy-five men aboard survived the initial bombing raid and flew on to mainland China, where darkness and low fuel caused four of the planes to ditch and others to parachute out. The survivors were protected by Chinese villagers and guided through the enemy-held territory. Tens of thousands of Chinese were killed by the Japanese because they would not give up the locations of the American pilots.

Not everyone accepted Jimmy Doolittle's offer to be part of his operation. Some even initially signed on and later realized that the danger was more than they wanted to take on. In the end, less than one hundred crewmembers signed on and as it turned out, that was more than enough.

In business, we get discouraged that we have a tough time finding good people to lead. It is usually the one we expect the most from who disappoints, and the one we expect the least from shows great promise. The example that we draw from Jesus and the apostles is that it is nice to have a large group cheering you on when things are going well, but it is equally good to have a loyal core around you when you face adversity and challenges.

Questions:

1. Why should people follow you?

2. Have you overlooked an individual on your business or organizational team?

3. Who in your life is with you, no matter what?

4. Who would you follow off of an aircraft carrier in the middle of the night, in an airplane not designed to take off from said carrier?

Notes

Chapter Seven

*I*n chapter seven, we find Jesus at home in Galilee with family and close friends. He is trying to avoid those who want to kill Him, so His plan is to lay low and stay out of Judea. Jesus is aware of the risks that He faces but those around Him do not. They want to give Him advice on what to do, without knowing the situation. He basically tells them that they can go and do what they want to because they are not in the same situation that He is. Jesus sticks to his guns and does not go to Judea at the time, even though His family and friends, who don't understand or believe His mission, urge Him to do so. A short time later, Jesus does go to Judea in secrecy, staying out of public view until the time is right. Sometime in the middle of the Festival of Shelters, Jesus makes His move and appears in the middle of the temple and begins teaching. The authorities are amazed at His knowledge and He openly confronts them regarding the Law of Moses and their intention to kill Him.

By speaking to the crowds, Jesus caused people to openly question if He was actually the Messiah. The authorities used scripture stating that the Messiah would come of the family of David and be born in Bethlehem, so how could Jesus be the Messiah when He came from Galilee!

This bit of misinformation caused half of the crowd to disbelieve Him. Many wanted Jesus arrested, but no one touched Him.

Chapter Seven Business Lesson

If you will recall, Jesus listened to His mother in regard to the timing of His ministry at the wedding of Cana. He knew that Mary would give Him good and loving advice. In chapter seven, the advice that Jesus got from the other family members was tainted with disbelief and was disingenuous. As much as it hurts to admit it, not everyone close to you is rooting for your business and personal success. Those closest to you may have no clue as to what you are up against and will give you all kinds of bad advice. As an example, a business owner or organizational leader has daunting responsibilities. It is possible that your friends and relatives have never written a large check for payroll taxes, health insurance, or business insurance. They may have never had to face monolithic governing agencies that seem only to exist to put you out of business, or had meet some other huge obstacle to business or organizational success. Take heart, this is what Jesus faced in the beginning of this chapter. His family and friends were giving Him advice regarding where to go and what to do without knowing all of the facts.

The next time you are at a family gathering and your cousin or sister-in-law starts to give you advice on what course of action your business or organization should take next, without knowing the facts, just remember that Jesus had to put up with the same stuff from His relatives.

In John 7:16, we find a great litmus test for leadership. A great leader is someone who defers compliments and glorifying words. In the case of a Christian business, the owner and managers must defer all of the glory to the Father, just as Jesus did. It is a current trend that secular business advice also encourages leadership to be humble and to defer praise to others. This is an interesting point because almost every self-help author or business guru offers advice that is rooted in scripture and they present it as their own original idea.

If you think about it, any movie or television show that features a bumbling boss always depicts a person who takes all of the credit and none of the blame. When they show a successful and competent leader, that person is humble, deferring credit for success and lifting up those that surround them. It looks like Hollywood agrees with Jesus on this point.

Lastly, we should never miss a life or business opportunity based on incorrect information. When the religious leaders failed to do their due diligence or ignored the found information regarding Jesus, they caused one half of the crowd to fall away from the belief that Jesus was the Messiah. It is important to note that they not only caused those in the crowd to disbelieve, but also caused many others to miss the Messiah to this day. The fact is that Jesus was born of the family of David and was born in the town of Bethlehem, thereby fulfilling the promise of scripture. Poor business and organizational planning decisions are made all the time based on incorrect and incomplete information and, as a result, many opportunities are missed.

According to a business study prepared at Ohio State University, business managers fail up to one half of the time when they make business decisions regarding their organization. The author of the study, Mr. Paul Nutt, a professor of management science, concluded that, "Enormous sums of money are being spent on decisions that are put to full use only half of the time." He states further that, "Managers need to look for better ways to carry out decision making." Falsely assuming a set of facts to be true has great and long-term implications in our business and organizational lives.

Questions:

1. Do you have people in your life that ask questions   or offer insights that help or hurt you in your business and organizational life?

2. How do you respond to them?

3. Think of the last business or organizationa decision that you made. Did you make that decision based on fact or emotion? What were the results of that decision, and were you satisfied?

Notes

Notes

Chapter Eight

*C*hapter eight starts with Jesus confronting an angry crowd that is about to stone a woman who was caught in the act of adultery. As the crowd disperses, Jesus forgives the woman's sin and sends her home. Next, He has a confrontation with the religious leaders regarding His ministry and purpose. The leaders attempt to catch Jesus in a lie, but He answers them with only the same truthful answers, confusing and angering them. In the remaining part of this chapter, Jesus speaks of freedom from sin being equal to freedom from slavery. He also confronts the hypocrisy that His enemies show in their actions and addresses who the devil is and what his role is in their confusion and disbelief. Their reactions to what He says are none too subtle, as they scream at Him and pick up rocks and stones to kill Him.

Chapter Eight Business Lesson

Organizations and business entities that are based on honesty and truthful practices will always have a free and unburdened work environment. Many times, I will see a business with a lofty mission statement and no action to back it up. As believers, we are to be constantly aware that our sinful nature, which is readily apparent to everyone, can cloud and distort the good intentions of a Christian business or organization. When we identify ourselves as such, we are open to much more scrutiny and attack. Claiming to be a Christian business or organization without the Christian faith in action is hypocrisy. The following example is a living testament of what Jesus is speaking of in this chapter.

In 1943, three World War II pilots met for prayer and bible study. During their time together they spoke of the need for aviation services designed for Christian missionaries located in remote locations around the world. For the missionaries who served in these areas around the globe, aviation services would change the mission fields forever. No more long boat trips, precarious backpack trips and burro journeys through treacherous enemy and disease-laden territories would be a welcome change. In 1944, one of those pilots, Jim Truxton, made plans to establish such a service after the war ended. In 1945, Christian Airmen's Missionary Fellowship was founded and is today known as Mission Aviation Fellowship. Currently, they operate out of my hometown of Redlands, California.

This organization could have been founded just so its members could get free flying hours and free trips to exotic places. After all, they could mask their real intentions to promote their aviation careers with a so called love for God and Christian missionaries. I am sure that in each of our lives we have seen so-called men and women of God who use their ministry, business or organization to promote their hobbies or lifestyle and can be regarded as disingenuous. In the case of this organization, their actions match their mission statement, that all people have access to both the Gospel and the resources to advance God's Kingdom. If you will go to the Mission Aviation website (http://www.maf.org/), you can read a complete historical account of this Godly organization, as well as see what their current activities are.

On January 8th, 1956, four missionary pilots were martyred for their faith in Jesus Christ. These men were entrusted to deliver the gospel to a savage tribe of people in Ecuador. They had unwittingly become involved in a tribal issue regarding its chief and he apparently invoked the village to participate in the killing of the missionaries. The pilots were armed and could have defended themselves, but did not, as they sacrificed their lives for their faith.

The tribal members were affected by the deaths of these missionaries. Most accepted Jesus Christ and were baptized in time. If those missionaries had opened fire on the tribe, it is possible that they could have survived, but their noble mission would have become ordinary. Lesser people, like myself, would have done everything they could to save themselves. All that would have done is validated to the tribe that there was limitations to what we believed and said.

When we state to the world that we are a Christian business, we are required to act like it at all times. If we put a Christian symbol on our business card or advertising, if we identify ourselves as being a Christian employer or promote ourselves as a Christian leader, we must be prepared to submit in faith as those missionaries did. If we react as the world dictates and not as Christ dictates, we fail to be the leader that God calls us to be. When the opportunity comes to use our righteous worldly weapons and we sue a business transgressor, undercut a competitor or employee, appear to be unfair to a customer or fail to be concerned for the welfare of those who work for us, we survive in a worldly sense but fail at our noble mission. If we follow Christ's example in our business practices, the world will be bewildered and confused by our actions. Like Christ's example, they will yell and scream and quite possibly pick up a rock or two to fling at you, but in the end, they may know Christ through you.

I should know because I have failed so many times and am grateful that God keeps giving me another chance to do it right.

In regard to the scrutiny and attacks, we must know who the devil is and how he thrives on lies and deceit. Many people that I know in business (including self-identified believers) look at me like I am crazy when I speak of the devil and how he will come against a Godly business plan. Jesus described the devil as a liar who hates the truth, a murderer and the father of all lies. The only defense we have is the truth of who Jesus Christ is.

Questions:

1. Does your business or organization have specific goals and positions?

2. Do the members of your business or organization make decisions based on those goals?

3. What happens when seemingly bad things result from making decisions based on those goals and ideals?

4. Have you developed, or are you part of a hypocritical organization.

5. What can you do about it?

Notes

Notes

Chapter Nine

$\mathcal{I}$n chapter nine, Jesus teaches us how to stand tall in the face of serious opposition. Whatever our position and place on earth is, God tells us to accomplish our tasks and act with urgency in all that we do. Jesus healed a blind man and the Pharisees attack Him again for healing on the Sabbath. The blind man who was healed was interviewed at great length by the religious leaders and grew frustrated at their repeated questions regarding who he thought Jesus was. He told them that he didn't know who Jesus was, but that he was blind his entire life and now he could see. This man was emboldened enough by his healing that he confronted the Pharisees with the fact that they were refusing to give credit to God for this miracle and he felt it was very strange that they would not believe their own eyes regarding his healing. This last observation got him tossed from the synagogue and denounced as a sinner.

Jesus found the man later and asked him if he believed in Him as the Son of God. He replied that he did. Jesus then told him that He came to judge the world, give sight to the blind and show those who think they can see that they are blind. The Pharisees heard what Jesus said and asked if He was saying that they were blind. Nothing got past these guys. Jesus responded that if they were blind, they would be guilt free, but the fact was that they remained guilty because they claimed to see.

Chapter Nine Business Lesson

When the Pharisees questioned among themselves whether Jesus came from God, there was a deep division of opinion among them. I can only assume that some of them were willing to entertain the idea that Jesus was who He said He was, as a result of seeing the miracle. Others refused to believe, despite the evidence before them. In business, your competitors and others who do not wish you success will see your inadequacies as a man or woman and question your Godly success. They will see the fruits of your Godly success and will deny them by telling you that you were just lucky and fortunate. Or they may take the other route and claim that you are crazy. Your fellow man may not deem you worthy, but God will.

In regard to business in America, there is no bigger business than the popular media business. This business includes music, video, television, the internet, movies and video games. This business is defined by the looks and personalities of the talent who write and perform the music, and act or support visual media behind the scenes. It is supported by layers of publications, television shows and stations, movie studios and graphic design studios, writers, personalities and reporters, radio stations and record companies. This business is united in thought like no other business. The basic message for at least the last fifty years is, trust no one, believe in nothing, have a good time, anarchy is good, sex, sex and more sex, men are bad, women are bad, revenge is cool, over the top violence is a good thing, men are pimps, women are hos, drugs and cigarettes are a staple of a life that isn't worth living and by the way, your parents and all those in authority have been, and still are, wrong about everything. I know that there have been uplifting movie and music hits that befuddle the powers that be in the entertainment business. But the general message distributed by all of the facets of this business are anything but mainstream and are influenced by secular, humanist beliefs, and the drive for money without regard to the damage done to our society. I will also note that if we didn't buy what they are selling, they wouldn't be in business. I should mention that there is one moral example that they are united behind, and that is stealing, from them. They are particularly upset when the fan base that they have developed steals their product and they lose their compensation. That is when the entertainment industry and their minions petition the very moral structure they have helped to destroy, to protect them and their royalty checks.

While writing this book, I became aware of the conversion to Christianity of a man by the name of Brian "Head" Welch, a hard rock guitarist in a band called Korn. Now for those of you, like me, who don't know the type of music Korn plays, this conversion is nothing short of a modern miracle. To say that Korn plays some nasty music is like saying that the Grand Canyon is just a hole in the ground.

The lyrics to the music of this group are disturbing and full of perverted, psychopathic and paranoid images that sport titles like "Freak on a Leash" and "Make Me Bad". Anyone who would perform in this band would be the very last living person to speak on behalf of God, but speak he did, as Brian addressed an audience of 10,000 at a church in California. There he spoke of how, at his lowest point, someone had given him a bible and that today he considers himself to be a happy man. To make sure that the world knew that he was sincere, Brian flew to Israel and was baptized in the Jordan River, an event that was covered in Rolling Stone magazine. I would like to make a point before I go on. The entertainment industry was, and is at this time, shocked that this man gave his life to Jesus. They write slyly that good old Brian might have a screw loose and somehow his life in the demented music scene wasn't anything but normal. These are the people that shape society and these are their values.

Jesus gives us an example of how important it is to stand up to those who oppose you and your business or organization. We cannot be disillusioned into believing that life is fair. The example of the Lord sticking to His guns in the face of opposition to His ministry gives us hope as we compete daily in our business lives. In this chapter, Jesus faced an opposition that thought they could wear Him down. The results of His effort refused them to succeed in their opposition.

When I accepted Christ in 1997, I was happy to share my newfound faith with everyone. As I shared that faith with family, friends and business clients, I watched them walk away and look at me like I was crazy. I was no longer able to look at business in cold, hard, free market economic terms and I interjected Jesus and the word of God into every bit of business advice and planning that I gave. To this day, I have lost contact with business and personal friends and associates because of my change in perspective. Like that blind man in the scripture or like Brian Welch, being tossed out and ignored isn't so bad as long as you have Jesus to replace your worldly losses.

Questions:

1. When was the last time you had to stand tall for your basic beliefs and or the goals and ideals of your business or organization?

2. Did you feel satisfied with the results?

3. Have you ever stood for something and had to pay a price?

4. Do others know what you stand for?

Notes

Notes

Chapter Ten

 $\mathcal{I}$ n chapters ten and eleven in the book of John, Jesus gives us an example of inspired leadership. It is important to note that He carved out His market share one act and one day at a time. Those around Him were looking for Him to be consistent in His actions, and He was aware that to grow His ministry, those who followed required constant attention and reassurance. In chapter ten, He speaks of how His followers know His voice and will follow it. Without that consistent voice, the mission would fail. Jesus also warned them that the voice of a thief or dishonest person is recognized as a person who wishes to only steal, kill and destroy. Jesus warns his followers to be discerning in whom they follow. He also calls upon His followers to believe only in Him if they can see that He is carrying out the work of the Father. In other words, accountability applies to both those who lead and those who follow.

Chapter eleven tells the story of Lazarus and how Jesus raised him from the dead. Throughout this chapter, the actions of Jesus match His previous core message and mission statement. His followers are both mystified and encouraged by His actions, words and miracles. As in previous chapters, Jesus faces constant opposition from the established religious leaders who are now starting to plot His murder.

Chapter Ten Business Lesson

Effective leaders inspire confidence among those who are being led. We recognize when our leaders are not being sincere or truthful and while we may go through the motions of following them, we don't. In my experience, employees or organizational members will follow a leader and remain committed to the organization until the day they recognize that the leader's words do not match his or her actions. We will follow leaders who have a voice that we recognize as truthful and can be measured against the word of God to verify its authenticity.

Secondly, we face challenges in our business life that will require great faith and will seem impossible. I have worked with many Godly business people who have faced insurmountable problems by doing all that they can do and relying on God to carry them through. Through Jesus Christ, we have great power to overcome impossible problems and challenges, something the secular world will not understand.

An example of such business leadership can be found in the life of James Cash Penney. Born on September 16, 1875, the seventh of twelve children, J C Penney was born into a Spartan existence. The son of poor but God fearing parents; he was raised on a farm near Hamilton, Missouri, and had a joyless and difficult young life. His father instilled self-reliance in young Penney and at the age of eight, he was told that he would have to buy his own clothes. In order to raise money, he bought a young pig, fattened it up and sold it for a profit, used to buy more pigs. Penney continued to reinvest his profits in more livestock and grew to appreciate his life as a budding entrepreneur.

Now, Mr. Penney went on to be a world famous businessperson who called his first retail establishment the "Golden Rule Store", which he founded in 1902. As the name implied, Penney "wished to do unto others and they would do onto you." He changed the face of the retail business in America forever. He operated his business and related to those around him as an honest, Godly man who developed a foundation of trust with his customers in a business world that made his actions contrary to the competition.

While competitors continued to show disdain for their customer base, Penney strived for honesty and fairness. Many of the services and courtesies that we expect to receive from a retail store, such as money back returns, quality merchandise, friendly customer service and fair pricing, were part of Mr. Penney's base business values and not found among any of his competition. It is also fair to note that Penney used the word of God as part of his business plan and was richly rewarded for it. Like his Christian business counterpart Henry Heinz, Penney listened to the Shepard and heard and followed His voice.

Penney went on to be a great benefactor to many charities and to society in general. Near the end of his life, having a position on the board of the company that bore his name, the board of directors voted to institute the J C Penney charge card. Mr. Penney cast the lone vote against the idea. His concern was that people would become too burdened and would have their lives affected in an adverse way if they were to take on debt through the use of a credit card. Mr. Penney died on February 12, 1971, leaving a legacy of business success, kindness and love for others, along with testimonial examples of how a man could follow God's word and be a huge success in a capitalist society.

In our business lives, we face crossroad decisions that will determine our success or failure in the future. As Christians, we listen for the voice of the Shepard as we make difficult business and organizational decisions. Without listening for that voice, we can make decisions that lack a sense of moral direction and can have an impact on the rest of our lives.

Going back to our example, when Mr. Penney was a young man, he moved his family to a new town and invested all of his money in a butcher shop. Part of the value of the butcher shop was that it was the exclusive supplier to the local hotel that used a considerable amount of meat in its dining room. When Penney went to service the account, the chef informed him that in order to keep his business, a bottle of whiskey was to accompany each weekly order.

Now, if I have just sunk all of my family's money into a butcher shop in an unfamiliar place, with a wife and children counting on me to make the right decision regarding their future and if I had to give some "snake in the grass" a bottle of whiskey now and again to keep his business, I would have done what Mr. Penney did and paid the bribe. Penney felt terrible about caving in on his principals. Even though he did it once, he refused to do it again, lost the account and the butcher shop and was dead broke in the middle of nowhere with a young family.

This Godly man knew what was right and because he had been raised as a believer in Jesus Christ, he listened for His voice and eventually made the right decision. In fact, he believed that all of his future success came from that decision and if he hadn't had the courage to do it, he might have been stuck being a small town butcher instead of becoming an American business icon.

Success depends on the most unspectacular of events, a place from which we launch our greatest victories and failures.

Questions:

1. Do the voices of the leaders in your business or organization ring true?

2. Does your business or organization follow the "Golden Rule"?

3. What do you hold as a core belief and does it match management or ownership's core beliefs?

4. Where have your past successes and failures pivoted on?

5. Do you listen for the voice of the Shepard?

Notes

Notes

Chapter Eleven

In the book of John, chapter twelve opens with Jesus enjoying time with his friends at a dinner in His honor at the home of Lazarus, the man Jesus raised from the dead. Lazarus enjoyed a great friendship with Jesus. With the help of his sisters, Mary and Martha, he put together a great feast for Jesus and His disciples. While Martha prepared to serve the food, Mary sat at the feet of the Messiah and washed His feet with an expensive perfume, and the house was filled with its fragrance. One of the apostles, Judas, got upset and complained that the perfume was expensive and was being wasted. He justified his complaint by saying that they could have sold the perfume and fed the poor. Jesus knew that the real motivation behind the objection was the apostle's self interest and told him to leave Mary alone because she was actually preparing the body of Jesus for burial.

The news that Jesus was at the home of Lazarus drew great crowds and really upset the religious authorities. They had seen a decrease in those who followed them as a result of the miracle involving Lazarus. The next day, a huge crowd of Passover visitors took palm branches and went to meet Jesus. The crowds were made up of many people who had seen the miracle involving Lazarus. Even more people arrived to see Jesus upon hearing the story recounted. When the religious leaders saw the amount of adulation shown by the crowd, they were disturbed and started to put their plan to kill Jesus into action.

The bible says that there were some Greeks who were in attendance and they requested to meet with Jesus. In response to their questions during the meeting, Jesus told them that He would be dying soon and explained the reason why, in a practical analogy. He explained that a kernel of wheat must be planted in the soil, where it must die alone. In the process of dying, the seed will produce many other seeds to create a bountiful harvest.

Next, the bible says that the crowd turned against Jesus. They forgot all of the acts of goodness He had done and had no memory of His miracles. Many people believed Jesus, including some of the Jewish leaders, but they kept their beliefs to themselves.

Chapter Eleven Business Lesson

Again, the picture of Jesus relaxing with friends and family should be an example of how we should live our daily lives. As the bible points out, Jesus was under a lot of pressure at this time in His life. He faced extreme resistance from others in the building of His church and ministry. He could have given us an example of a tireless, no nonsense and success driven organizational leader and manager who focused on business and success only. Instead, we are given a picture of a leader who undoubtedly enjoyed those that He worked with and spent time with. Business owners and organization builders can take heart and realize that this example teaches us to work hard when we are working and when we are done with that effort, be prepared to enjoy the results of that hard work with those that we enjoy being with.

I particularly appreciate the example of Mary anointing the feet of Jesus with expensive perfume. Not only did Mary bring comfort to Jesus, but the fragrance drifting through the house must have brought pleasure to everyone there that day. The impression that I have taken from this example is that God does not mind it if you spend some of the money that you make for things that may be considered luxurious or high end. The world, Christians included, may criticize successful and Godly business owners who buy something nice for themselves, their family, their friends or their business itself. Their complaint may echo Judas' and they may be critical, but I don't think God shares their point of view. The key to all of this is, are we living up to the "Godly" part? There is a difference between accumulating personal wealth and being blessed by providence. When Judas brought up the point about how the money for the perfume could have been used for the poor, he was disingenuous and gives a good example of how others who do not have your best interest at heart, may advise you from a "moral" standpoint. I am positive that there are many people who have rejected God simply because they believe that only the poor can know Him. Don't forget, God created diamonds, rubies and the raw materials that go into the making of this year's Cadillac or Mercedes.

Secondly, when things are going well, don't get caught up in the adulation of those around you. As quickly as they adore you, the quicker they will turn on you when you hit a rough patch. During the time when everyone was laying palm branches at His feet, His competition, the religious leaders, were plotting to kill Him. Those who were cheering for Him at this time were screaming for His death not long after. The example that Jesus gives is one in that He seems to go along with the crowd on the surface and stays on target in achieving organizational goals in practice. You really need to be an effective leader to keep your eye on the target and not let the euphoria or despair of others to distract you from your stated plan.

Thirdly, part of the investment we make in a successful business or organization are the lonely hours of toil that are never reflected in the light of success. Most people will look at a successful businessperson and attribute much of their success to timing and luck. Observers never want to account for the "dying hours" that took place during the start-up phase of the business or organization. From a business or organizational standpoint, the example that Jesus gives regarding the death of a seed that is planted is necessary so as to allow other seeds to grow out of that planting. A practical example of this would be the building of a house. Everyone will give you advice regarding the color of paint, furniture, plants, wallpaper, appliances and even the type of television to buy because these items are of interest to everyone. The part of construction that is boring and of little interest to anyone are the "dying hours" spent digging the foundation that the house will sit on. It's not very exciting building a foundation, simply because the essential effort gets covered up. If it is done right, it is never thought of again. On the other hand, if it isn't done right, it will have a detrimental effect on the structure of the house forever.

Jesus knew that His life and death were a foundational necessity and without His investment, there would be no church. The reason that so many new business ventures fail within the first year is because the person starting the business is not willing to invest those "dying hours" in the beginning. They don't have the patience needed to harvest the success that takes time to materialize. If we are to "grow" success in our business or organization, we must invest our time and effort in these mundane and foundational efforts.

Questions:

1. When was the last time you were able to enjoy the company of those closest to you? To enjoy food, conversation and just plain relax?

2. Have you or have you known anyone who has rejected God because of the belief that you must be poor to be faithful?

3. Do you believe that God brings blessings to a business or individual so that they may be a blessing to others?

4. Have you ever gotten caught up in the adulation of others at one moment only to be criticized by the same people later?

5. Have you committed to or have you already invested in the "dying hours" necessary for the foundation of your business or organization?

Notes

Chapter Twelve

*I*n chapter thirteen and fourteen of the book of John, Jesus gives us an example of strength in leadership through an act of humility by washing the feet of His apostles. The bible says that Jesus knew what tribulations were before Him and again, He wanted to spend time with His management team to reinforce His core beliefs on their ministry.

When Jesus went to Peter, the apostle was reluctant to have Jesus perform such a menial task and objected loudly. When Jesus explained that the washing of the feet symbolized Peter's own relationship with Jesus forever, the apostle asked that Jesus not only wash his feet but his whole body. When Peter found out what God had in mind, he didn't want to miss any of it.

After washing the feet of the apostles, Jesus sat down and asked if they understood what He was doing. He explained that He was giving them an example of how to treat one another and that if they followed the core values of the ministry; they would be successful and happy.

At this point in the word, Jesus predicts that He will be betrayed and denied by those in that very room. The apostles were disturbed by this and started to get a little upset. Jesus calmed them by telling them that it would be all right because He was going ahead to prepare a place for them for eternity in His Father's house. It is striking that even after the apostles traveled with Jesus, saw the miracles, heard the words and looked into his eyes, they still didn't quite understand everything He was telling them.

Despite the fact that they didn't understand the complete vision of Christ at that time, He promised that He would send the Holy Spirit to help them in the future. In the book of Acts, we see the fulfillment of this promise. The fainthearted and timid men in this chapter become mighty managers and builders of the faith. All, with the exception of John, died lonely and painful deaths, and none of them denied their faith in Jesus Christ.

Chapter Twelve Business Lesson

As managers and organizational leaders, the human instinct is to be honored, not to honor others. Imagine a captain of industry going around and washing the feet of his or her board of directors. The world that we live in requires us to be strong and forceful. If a business leader did try to wash the feet of those at the board meeting, the news would be reported immediately and everyone would sell his or her stock because it was obvious that the CEO had lost his or her mind. While we may not use this example of management servitude, we may opt to be kind and courteous to those who work for us and make an effort so that, as in Christ's example, others may see strong, inspired and compassionate leadership. Just prior to washing the feet of the apostles, Jesus asked everyone at the meeting if they truly understood His instructions and what they were trying to accomplish as an organization. It has been my experience as a manager and owner that if a project goes south, it's because I or someone else failed to take the time to communicate with staff members. Mind reading is a skill that may be useful if you work in a carnival, but how many times have you sat in a meeting and just did not understand what was going on because the speaker was being sketchy with details and avoiding the point? How many times have you made a presentation and your audience just didn't get it? The example that Jesus gives us is to be direct with the information, even if it is difficult or scary. People, as in the example of the apostles, will make up their own minds as to whether they can do their part.

The funny thing is, everyone knows that it is effective to show yourself as a compassionate and serving leader. Years ago, my company provided public relations services to a large local business that made a big show out of feeding the homeless once a year in a local park. The members of the board, the CEO and the local assortment of politicians and public figures dutifully served up food and smiled at the recipients while the television cameras rolled and the reporters were present. When the last camera and reporter left, they dropped their serving utensils and prearranged food servers took over. I am always struck at how good we are as humans to pantomime good behavior. The employees who were present saw these real reactions and used them as a filter to process future communications and directives from management

It takes a great manager to appear subservient to those under them. It is very possible that members of your management team and even employees themselves will view a caring manager or supervisor as weak, but the majority will follow with great loyalty.

Secondly, there will be people who are part of your organization who will be disloyal to you and what you stand for and will certainly betray you. If it can happen to the Son of God, it can happen to you. This will cause you a great deal of distress when it happens and will cause you to question everything and everyone in your organization. The betrayal of Jesus was essential to complete God's plan. Bad things happen in businesses and organizations, and out of the betrayal will come a stronger business or organization. When these bad things happen, we only have two choices; let it derail us and cause us to spiral downward or have a short "pity party", saddle up and move on. Teddy Roosevelt had a great quote, "Do what you can, with what you have, where you are."

Thirdly, as Peter was put in the position to deny Christ, in our daily business lives, we will too. Several years ago, my company produced a film for a large military museum in Southern California.

The director of the museum worked very close with us in regard to the content and arranging interview sessions with people who were eyewitnesses to the historical events depicted in the documentary. We had a special viewing for the board members of the museum who, with the director herself, gave the film a hearty endorsement.

Prior to the public release of the film, the museum director and I were discussing the distribution plans and the conversation moved to where she wanted to know where I got my inspiration for the project. I told her that I believed that all inspiration came from God and she explained that she was also spiritual. I then asked her if she knew Jesus Christ as her Lord and Savior. I can't describe the look she gave me. Her face actually twisted in a way I didn't think humanly possible. All she said before she got up and left me at the meeting table was, "I am a white witch and I am very spiritual!" Her look and attitude said that she wasn't interested in hearing about who Jesus was. She shelved my film, removed all support from it and we never sold a copy. She never spoke to me again. Although I was disappointed and confused by her reaction from a business standpoint, I have never looked back with regret or wished I had said something different. Many times I questioned God as to why He would allow me to spend so much time working on that project and have it not show any financial fruit. I have come to the conclusion that maybe He just wanted me to share the name of Jesus with that person, that day.

Lastly, the same things the Holy Spirit promised to the apostles is promised to us. Before I accepted Jesus Christ as my personal Savior, business and organizational responsibilities caused a lot of pressure and concern in my life. I worried about payroll, where our next project would come from or what I was going to do next. It took me four years to believe the promise of God and piece by piece I turned my worries and concerns over to the Holy Spirit. Since that time, I have had peace in my business and personal life. My life is not perfect, I still work hard and face as many setbacks as before, the difference being how I handle it. I am thankful for

God in my daily business life.

Questions:

1. Are those around you worthy of honor?

2. How do you or how could you honor others in your organization?

3. Can you and have you forgiven those who have betrayed you in the past?

4. Do you make sharing the Word of God to be part of your business plan?

5. Have you and can you turn your business and personal life over to Jesus Christ?

Notes

Chapter Thirteen

The entire content of chapter fifteen in the book of John is attributed to the words of Jesus. He speaks of the parable of the vine, how He is the true vine and His Father is the gardener. He also speaks of how we are the branches on the vine as His followers, and the importance of pruning the vine for maximum growth. We are encouraged to remain joined to Him because if we are apart from Him, we cannot produce fruit.

Jesus then speaks as to how He loves us like the Father loves Him, and commands us to love one another. An example of the greatest love we can show is laying down our lives for each other. Our previous example of the Mission Aviation martyrs exemplifies this teaching. He then goes on to explain that when we face resistance and rejection because we follow Him, those who reject us, hated Him first. It makes sense that if they persecuted Him, they will persecute us.

He closes out this chapter by giving marching orders to the apostles, telling them to, "Tell others about me because you have been with me from the beginning."

Chapter Thirteen Business Lesson

To start with, Jesus gives us a basic business premise to apply in reference to the trimming of the vineyard. If we look at our personal habits, employees or organizational staff members, customers or clients and then ask the question "do they or does it produce fruit?" we will make wise business and organizational moves and corrections. We must look at this from both a practical and a faithful position. We are called to be faithful and diligent in the changes we make in regard to our business so that as a result of our pruning, the business or organization should grow.

A Godly business owner or manager is required to make necessary changes to their business or organization so that they can continue to succeed and grow. Others may be critical and say that as a Christian, you are required to keep unproductive people, attain little or no profit and run your business or organization without economic goals and guidelines. Jesus Himself allowed many of His followers to leave His early organization and He set (and still sets) uncompromising standards that we have to meet if we are to serve with Him. God calls us to be good stewards and to use every asset that He gives us for the betterment of His kingdom. In that quest for stewardship, lazy people get fired, those who steal get prosecuted and those who fulfill their organizational and work related duties are blessed and rewarded through the Godly success of the business or organization.

Secondly, when we identify our business or organization as Christian, be prepared for adversity. Jesus tells us to remember that the world hated Him first and will in turn hate us. If there is any doubt in your mind about this, think about the last movie that you saw. Did you notice when it came time for blasphemy to come out of the mouth of an actor, which name came out? In fact they do it so much that they have given Jesus the middle initial "H". When God commands us to not use His name in vain, He is telling us that there is power in the calling out of His name. When we use the name of God in a vain way, we waste that power. If scriptwriters really understood what they are doing when they use God's name in vain, and if the actors could get a glimpse of the power of God, we would never hear God's name used like that in a movie, book or personal conversation again.

Scriptwriters don't write the names of Buddha or Mohammad when they want to blaspheme, they always write in the name of Jesus. When the ACLU attacks a religion, they are consistent. They only attack Christ and Christians. I can't recall them going after Islamic or Hindu icons, only Christ and His followers. I believe the reason that the world isn't critical of the other religions mentioned is that they fear that the followers of those religions may threaten or hurt them for being disrespectful. When we identify ourselves as a Christian business or organization, we are bound by our faith to bear witness, so that everything we do reflects Christ, including the tolerance and forgiveness of our enemies. Will we do this everyday without fail? Sadly, no as I literally fail every day in this, I repent and try again.

Thirdly, every Christian business and organization shares the commission that Christ gave His apostles at the end of this chapter. According to His word, we have known Him from the beginning and we are required to tell others about our faith so that they may know Him, too.

Each business day, we meet people who are hurting. We are exposed to the problems that our employees face in their private lives, customers and clients share their deepest concerns regarding their business and personal lives and strangers with unique problems are placed in our business and professional lives every day. We must be prepared to pray with them and be willing to be the distributors of God's love each and every time. So when you identify your organization as Christian or you place the symbol of a fish on your business cards, you "mark" yourself and incur additional Godly responsibilities.

Questions:

1. When was the last time that you trimmed your "vineyard"?

2. Can you and have you forgiven those who have betrayed you in the past?

3. If you do, how do you do it?

4. If you don't, why is that?

5. When was the last time that you prayed with a customer or a member of your organization?

Notes

Notes

Chapter Fourteen

*C*ontinuing in the book of John, chapter sixteen starts with a warning from Jesus that, as His followers, we will face rejection from the world that we are a part of. He told the apostles that they would be expelled from the synagogues and the time will come when people will kill His followers under the belief that they are fulfilling the word of God. Christ then promises that the Holy Spirit will be among His followers and that the Spirit of Truth will convict the world and encourage the believers.

In this passage, Jesus makes mention of the fact that judgment will take place because the devil exists in the world and that he has been judged.

Next, the apostles were more than a little confused when Jesus told them that He was leaving soon and then opened the floor up to questions regarding where He was going to go to. Jesus answered their specific questions and gave an analogy about childbirth and how pain can bring joy. He then gave specific instructions on how to pray and ask for favor from God the Father. Because Jesus spoke directly and not in parables to the apostles, they finally understood that Jesus was and is God. At the end of this chapter, Jesus explained to the apostles that they would be scattered and face the trials and tribulations of this world after He was gone.

Chapter Fourteen Business Lesson

In the first century, Christians suffered intense persecution. When two Christians would meet, one would make a mark in the dirt or sand in the shape of a half circle while the other would make a similar mark above it, thereby creating what looked like the figure of a fish. This was the way the members of the persecuted church could identify each other quietly and, with the move of a hand or foot, the "fish" could quickly be erased. In America, we are able to openly state our faith and many business people put the Christian symbol of a fish on every piece of advertising, from business cards to stationery. With the use of the Christian symbol, a business opens themselves up to rejection and judgment from a world that will see the fish symbol identifying you as a Christian business. The rejection will come from believers and nonbelievers or people who have had bad experiences in the past with other business people who had a fish on their calling card. It will come from those who see the symbol as an opportunity to challenge your Christian values because they see it as a sign of weakness and vulnerability. Judgment will come from those who evaluate your efforts in relation to the teachings of God.

When a business operates under the authority and inspiration of the Holy Spirit, it can thrive and survive as an identifiable Christian business. As an example of how this can be done, I would like to tell you about a business that is an institution in Southern California and is owned and operated by a Godly family.

In 1948, a man by the name of Harry Snyder opened what is considered the first drive through hamburger stand. He named it In-N-Out. He built the business on the basis of quality fast food, a simple menu and customer service. Unlike most of the drive through chains that copied In-N-Out, Mr. Snyder developed a following of regular customers who were, and still are, willing to wait in line for as long as fifteen minutes at peak periods of the day.

From a business standpoint, In-N-Out is considered a huge success.

The company has over 140 locations in California, Nevada and Arizona and is still growing. The thing that separates this company from others is the way they operate in faith. This family has made it a point to treat their more than 7,000 employees well and to create a work environment that is based on the love of Jesus Christ. The starting wage is $8.00 per hour with paid vacations, free meals and a 401k plan. Full time employees are eligible for medical insurance benefits. The average store manager earns $80,000 per year and most of them start out as hourly employees. Not only is the food great, I am impressed with the attitude of the employees every time I visit an In-N-Out.

Since this business has remained family owned and operated, they are free to share their faith through the printing of bible verses on their serving cups and wrappers. The soda cups bear the notation John 3:16, the milkshake cups list Proverbs 3:5 and Nahum 1:7 and Revelations 3:20 is featured on the hamburger wrappers. All of these bible verses promote belief in Jesus Christ as Lord.

In reference to what Jesus said about the devil being in this world, I have found that many deny his existence and many others want to blame him for everything wrong in their lives. Regarding this Godly company, a case can be made for the devil's existence in our world and his coming against them.

In 1976, Rich Snyder, one of two sons of the founders, Harry and Esther Snyder, took the position of President at the age of 24. During his tenure as President, the company grew from 18 to 93 locations. Richard died in a plane crash in 1993 and his brother, Guy Snyder, took the position of Chairman of the Board and CEO and oversaw further growth to 140 locations by the time of his accidental death in 1999. Esther Snyder currently manages the business, as she serves in the position of President.

Despite the worldly success that this family owned business has attained, the amount of success in faith they have achieved can be measured by the impact that they have made in the lives of their employees, the effort to share the word of God with their customers and the amount of pain and resistance they have been subjected to by the evil one. I believe that evidence of the Holy Spirit exists in this company today.

As terrific as this example of a Godly company is, there are many more business owners who operate with a fish plastered everywhere in their advertising, and Christian principals are nowhere to be found in their business practices. Truth in advertising is critical when it comes to representing the Lord in your business or organization.

The final words in the chapter tell us to take heart, because Jesus has overcome this world and when we operate along side Him, we do to.

Questions:

1. Is God part of your multimedia marketing plan?

2. Do you currently do business with someone who exalts God in his or her advertising or daily business practices?

3. What is your reaction when you see references to God and His word in a business' marketing message?

4. Does your business message match up with God's word?

Notes

Notes

Chapter Fifteen

*C*hapter seventeen of the book of John is almost a complete narrative from Jesus regarding how He views His responsibility towards His disciples and believers. Jesus defers to the Father all throughout this chapter. He speaks about how He presented the Father and His word in every possible way, and that He was an example of that word in everything that He did. Jesus says that He did not pray for the world in general, but for those who have been entrusted to Him by the Father. Jesus also points out that the world will hate those who follow Him, and that He doesn't ask the Father to remove the followers from the world but instead to protect them from the evil one while they are part of the world

Jesus goes on to say that He is praying for all believers in Him who have chosen to believe as a result of the testimony of the apostles. He stresses the connection that exists between the Father and the believer, and how His job is to convey the Father's word and love so that we may have interaction with our creator.

Chapter Fifteen Business Lesson

In the years that I engaged in business consulting, I always analyzed the type of management style and values used by ownership and/or upper management. It has been my experience that in a majority of cases, business owners and managers learned their management skills from their father or a father-like mentor who trained them along the way during their career. When we look at business management from a historical perspective, the great managers and business builders of their day (J C Penney, Henry Heinz, etc.) took a paternalistic approach toward their employees and took to heart what Christ had to say in chapter seventeen. A paternalistic approach to management, without understanding and putting into action what Christ teaches us in this chapter, is simply a hollow management style. In the cases of Penney and Heinz, and in the previous example of the Snyder family at In-N-Out, you could see trace evidence of God and His word in their business and see the fruit of their faith in their daily actions.

Business and employment opportunities have changed so much since I graduated from high school in the late 1960's. At that time, a young man or woman could find a job at an automobile plant or refinery, go to work for a phone company or some other type of a utility company or walk onto a construction site and apply for work. When we went to work, we went with the implied understanding that we and the management/ownership were in it for the long haul and that the chances were very good that we would, in theory, retire from that very job. The business environment up until that period probably didn't even know that they were in agreement with the Lord in chapter seventeen.

In the middle of this chapter, Jesus states that others will believe in Him because they believe the example of the apostles. It was so important for those who followed Jesus to see His righteous example every day so that they could speak to others with conviction. The integrity and fortitude of these "managers" were as essential to the success of the work of God as anything else Jesus did during His ministry on earth. Those who manage in the biblical example set forth in this chapter will not only be successful in this world, but will be honored before God Himself.

Lastly, a healthy and good Christian business will be identified and represented well by all of its employees. They understand and believe in the business and will reflect the ownership/

management's core values of the business. We can't force this to happen; it either exists or it doesn't.

Questions:

1. Do we cultivate loyalty in our business or organization by caring for the needs of those who are subordinate to us?

2. Which is more dangerous for you to do from a business standpoint: show compassion, vulnerability and love to those in your business or organization or just jump into a tank of water filled with man-eating sharks?

3. When you show compassion and care for others, what do you expect to get in return and from whom?

4. In regard to employees and management, how deep do the core values of the business or organization go?

Notes

Chapter Sixteen

*C*hapter eighteen of the book of John opens with Jesus and the disciples in the olive grove, located in the Kidron valley, where Judas will betray Him. The bible says that Jesus spent a lot of time with the apostles in this area, and Judas knew it would be easy to track Him there.

The religious leaders came loaded for bear. They brought along a battalion of Roman soldiers, the Temple Guards and an assortment of weapons, all to arrest one man. When they arrived Jesus stepped forward and asked them who they were looking for. When they told Him, He identified Himself. The bible says (in another book) that Peter reacted to this show of force and severed the ear of one of the servants of the high priest.

As they took Jesus away to the courtyard to be questioned by the high priest, Peter was allowed to follow into the courtyard and denied, for the first time, that he knew Jesus. During the questioning, the high priest asked Jesus about His basic teachings. Jesus told him and the others that what He had said was well documented and that there were plenty of people around who could confirm His teachings and message. Soon after this exchange, the high priest sent Jesus on to his superior, the high priest Caiaphas for trial. It is during this time that Peter denied knowing Jesus for the second and third time.

After Caiaphas was through talking to Jesus, he turned Him over to the Roman governor, Pontius Pilate. The bible insinuates that the religious leaders turned Jesus over to the Romans, because the Romans could execute a person while Jewish law did not allow capital punishment. When Pilate called for Jesus to come before him to be judged, he asked Jesus if He was the King of the Jews. Jesus responded with another question, asking Pilate if this was an idea that came to him personally or was he asking because others told him this? Pilate flipped out and Jesus went on to explain that He was a king, just not an earthly king. He explained further that if He were a king of this world, His army would have freed Him when He was arrested. Jesus went on to explain that He was born to fulfill the role of king, to bring truth into the world and those who recognized truth would recognize Him. Pilate then turned toward the crowd and offered to free a prisoner, according to tradition, because Jesus didn't seem to be all that bad. He was surprised when the crowd chanted for the release of a convicted murderer instead.

Chapter Sixteen Business Lesson

All businesses face trials and tribulations. Much of my time in the consulting business was spent negotiating with state and federal tax collectors, municipal service providers and general business creditors. The reason for this was simple. No business needs a consultant when things are going well. They called upon me as a last resort, in most cases. I was always struck with the different attitudes of those I negotiated with, as some were very reasonable and some were not so reasonable. As an example, I found federal tax collectors willing to make a deal, while state tax collectors were less than tolerant. Suppliers usually let me work out a plan for repayment that allowed the client to buy raw materials so they could continue production, and I found that the utility companies were less than forgiving and quite willing to shut the whole business down if they didn't get paid.

My purpose in bringing this up is to illustrate a daily example of how business owners are under extreme pressure. They face many accusers, who can appear overpowering, and have the full weight of the law on their side. Jesus was accused without merit and He gives us an example of how to face these trials and hardships. When you read this chapter, you will realize that Jesus met His accusers head on. I never get a sense that Jesus had His eyes down in a meek position. Instead, when they gave Him a loaded question, He gave them a truthful and straightforward answer that they didn't want to hear. He gave us an example of how to face adversity.

A businessperson will always face problems, it comes with the territory. A businessperson who identifies him or herself as a Christian businessperson brings greater scrutiny. We as Christian business owners can mess up as well as anybody and our critics are good at pointing out our real and imagined failures. How a business is perceived through the actions of ownership and their employees can in fact deny Christ and Christian principles. The important part is not what we have done in the past, but what we do now (repent) and in the future (do what is right). When the apostles scattered and Peter denied Christ, they didn't give the greatest example to other believers or to the rest of the unbelieving world. In fact, it looked pretty grim if you were a follower of Jesus Christ at that time.

When we are in crisis, it helps if everyone is clear about the core values of the business or organization, what the base message is and the strength of our personal beliefs and the forthrightness of the organizational leader. After the apostles failed in this chapter, we see later that they returned to the core values that were established by Jesus and continued in their ministry. All of the apostles were murdered for their faith, with the exception of John, and they all died lonely, painful deaths. None of them denied Christ again. The apostles were able to do this because of the reasons outlined above and most importantly, their leader followed through on His word and proved that He was who He said He was and did what He said He would do.

Leadership and integrity in action.

Questions:

1. Do others in your organization or business believe what you say?

2. Are you clear in your "core value" message to others?

3. What proof do you have that those core values exist?

4. Regarding the last time that you faced adversity: where did it come from and how did you react?

Notes

Notes

Chapter Seventeen

*I*n John, chapter nineteen opens with Pilate ordering his soldiers to beat Jesus with a lead tipped whip. A crown of thorns is pressed into His head and He is presented to the crowd. During this torture Jesus is mocked and denigrated. When He is brought before the mob they shouted for His death. Jesus was asked if He understood that Pilate held control over His life or death. Jesus replied that Pilate had limited power and that power came from others, particularly the religious leaders who insisted on His murder. Pilate tried to release Jesus and the religious leaders said that if that happened, they would report him to Rome as a traitor against Caesar. Pilate then made the decision to turn Jesus over to the soldiers and the crowd to be crucified.

It is said that Jesus, after bearing His own cross, was crucified at a place called Skull Hill just out of town. Two criminals were crucified on each side of Him. Pilate posted a sign above Him that was written in Hebrew, Latin and Greek that said, "Jesus of Nazareth, the King of the Jews". The religious leaders wanted the sign changed to read, "He said, I am the King of the Jews", but Pilate rejected their request for a change. The soldiers then threw dice for His robe as His mother and disciples watched Him dying on the cross. When Jesus saw His mother Mary and His disciples, He appointed the apostle John to care for His mother after His death. Chapter nineteen says that Jesus cried out in thirst and was given a sponge soaked in sour wine to drink and soon after said "It is finished!" and gave up His spirit. The soldiers wished to hasten the deaths and broke the legs of the two criminals, thereby causing suffocation. When they came to Jesus, they realized that it wasn't necessary to break His bones as He had expired. So they pierced His side so that blood and water would flow out of Him.

There was a wealthy man by the name of Joseph of Arimathea, who was a secret follower of Jesus. He petitioned Pilate to allow him to release the body of Jesus to him for burial in a new tomb that he owned. Pilate gave him permission and Jesus was buried on the last day of preparation for Passover and a large stone was placed over the burial place.

Chapter Seventeen Business Lesson

When I started my independent business life I started with a vision and in my vision I only saw only good things. During my business life I tripped over all of the negative things that I failed to see initially. The things that I ran across that weren't fair appalled me and made me feel helpless. The people, who have failed me and those that I have failed, have been and always will be shameful parts of theirs and my human legacy. I have walked into business deals blindly with nothing but hope to secure success and have faced the consequences.

In the case of Jesus, He knew everything that was going to happen to Him long before it happened. He was truly innocent. Even those who denied Him then, as well as now, would have to agree that He didn't do anything to deserve what was done to Him.

To this day you will find those that ignore Jesus and what He did for us in this selfless act of sacrifice. To prove this point let us look at a recent film by Mel Gibson called "The Passion of the Christ". This movie earned an ironic "R" rating based on the violence shown during the depiction of Christ's suffering and death. Critics of the movie felt that its release would cause great problems between Christians and Jews stating that the movie was nothing more than a latter day "passion play" designed to cause hatred and hard feelings.

The movie was released in the Aramaic language and Gibson took on quite a risk in regards to his money and reputation. Several studios turned down the project and along with independent film distributor, Newmarket Films, Gibson had to develop an interesting alternative marketing plan to develop an interest in the movie. The "Passion" as it has become known, grossed over $370 million dollars in the United States and was honored as the film of the year by grateful U.S. movie theater owners, won the Faith and Values Award (a Christian movie award) at the Awards Gala and Report to the Entertainment Industry and The Peoples Choice Award but failed to get any recognition with the Hollywood elite. In fact, Oscar voters admitted that they hadn't even seen the film so as to form an educated opinion. They did choose a winner from movies that celebrated assisted suicide, the life history of a sexual statistician, a female pioneer in the field of abortion and an accounting of an American billionaire's eccentric life. All of which had grossed a total of just over $55 million dollars at that point in time.

Things haven't changed much since the time of the bible. Those that deny who Christ is do so out of laziness, anger and ignorance. Imagine the courage it would have taken for someone who is part of the elite to take up the case for Jesus. Can you imagine the power that the devil has over our so called "entertainment industry". The good news is that, like the devil on the day of Christ's death, the enemies of faith are spiritually blind. After all, despite decades of an abortion law shoved down their throats, people know in their hearts that the killing of the innocent is wrong. They also know that the so called "sexual revolution" did nothing to make society better. They also know that deep in their hearts that "mercy" killing by starvation and dehydration are intrinsically wrong, no matter what Hollywood says.

If the devil had spiritual vision and was as smart as he thinks he is, he would have done everything that he could have to stop Jesus from dying on the cross and rising from the dead thereby fulfilling Messianic prophecy.

No matter what you think of Mel Gibson and his movies, we have to admire the faith based business example that he gave us in the case of "The Passion of the Christ".

The last point that I would like to make is that we must have a succession plan in place so that our business or organization can go on after we are gone. In the case of Jesus, He had a deliberate management plan in place with the remaining apostles and we know that it was the right plan because it obviously worked. He also had a plan to take care of His mother when he entrusted her care to the apostle John. This may seem to be an insignificant point at first but I believe that God recorded everything in the bible for our benefit and a succession plan was definitely in place when He died.

Questions:

1. Can you relate something in your business or organizational life that required you to take financial risks for your faith?

2. What can you do in faith to promote Godly values in the entertainment industry? Are you inclined to make a phone call, write a letter or email to express your opinion?

3. Does any of your business or organizational expenditures offer financial support to those that are at odds with God's message?

4. Do you have a succession plan in place for your business or organization?

5. In the event of your death have you provided for surviving family members who count on your income and financial support?

Notes

Notes

Chapter Eighteen

*C*hapters 20 and 21 of the book of John give an accounting of the resurrection of Jesus and a record of the visitations that He had with the apostles. The bible says that the followers of Jesus went to visit the tomb where Jesus was buried. When they arrived, the stone front was removed and the tomb was empty. Fearing that the body was stolen they alerted the apostles who came running at the news. The burial clothes were still there but the body was gone and the apostles really started to get the hang of the resurrection promise that Jesus told them about.

The apostles went home and left Mary Magdalene, a follower of Jesus, at the tomb. She was upset and peered into the tomb to see for herself that the body was no longer there. While looking in, she saw two angels sitting where the body had been placed yesterday. Because she had tears of sadness, they asked her why she was upset. She answered that someone had stolen Jesus' body and she didn't know where they moved it. As she turned, she caught movement out of the corner of her eye her and recognized that it was Jesus. The bible says that she then ran to tell the apostles that she had seen Jesus.

Now the apostles reassembled some time later in a locked room fearful of the authorities and suddenly appearing in their midst was Jesus. Jesus showed them the wounds in His hands and they were overjoyed to see Him. Because Thomas the apostle wasn't present he was skeptical of the others account of meeting Jesus and said that he wouldn't believe until he could put his own hands into the wounds of Christ. Jesus obliged him at the next meeting with the apostles. When he did touch the wounds Jesus told him to be faithless, no longer. Jesus also said that we are blessed because we believe without seeing the wounds.

Later, the apostles went fishing on the Sea of Galilee and caught nothing the entire night. Now the apostles saw someone on the beach and heard him yell out a question as to how many fish they had caught. When they replied that they had caught nothing, he told them to try lowering their net on the other side and when they did, their net was full. At this time the apostles recognized it was Jesus on the shore and Peter jumped into the water, swimming to meet him. As the apostles came to shore they found Jesus cooking them breakfast over an open fire

After breakfast, Jesus challenged Peter to be the leader he was capable of being, informed him that he would suffer a martyrs death and that he was to care for the followers of Christ.

Chapter Eighteen Business Lesson

Jesus told everyone, enemies and friends alike, that after three days He would rise from the grave. There is an old saying, "It ain't bragging if you can do it". Part of the reason that His followers were so shocked was because of the tight security that the Romans installed so that the body of Jesus would stay put.

In our business life, if we make promises, we better deliver because people are naturally skeptical and they have been lied to by better people than you and I. If we claim to be a person of faith, we had better deliver, because the faith of others depends upon our actions.

The apostles, Peter in particular were not ready to be managers until they finally saw the proof that the Lord provided. Prior to the resurrection they were timid and afraid, locked up in a room trying their best to avoid confrontation with their enemies. Once they saw who Jesus was and when they realized that he was God, they went forward and as I mentioned before, they all died terrifying lonely deaths. John was the only one to survive after they tried to boil him in oil. All any of the apostles would have had to do would be to cry out that it was all a joke and that they made up the story of the risen Lord and they would have been pulled from the torture, cleaned up and allowed to live a long life denying that Jesus was God. But none of them did because they knew the truth.

In our business and organizational life, those who associate with us watch constantly to see if we walk our faith. If you do, they will follow you with the enthusiasm of a Peter jumping out of a boat to meet you on the shore.

That enthusiasm is a result of great leadership.

The very last thing I would like to share with you is the picture of the Lord of the universe cooking a fish and bread breakfast for his leadership team. As He has done all through this book of the bible Jesus showed how much He loved people and He loved being with them. Like I have said before, God gave us His word so that we would know how to live a fulfilled life both in a business and personal sense. So why not just take someone to breakfast and tell them about Jesus?

Questions:

1. Have you ever spoken prophetically?

2. Was the prophecy fulfilled?

3. Do we make promises in our business and   organizational life? Do we fulfill them?

4. Who is the most enthusiastic person in your business or organization?

5. When was the last time you took someone to breakfast to tell them about Jesus?

Notes